Religious Beliefs

ISSUES

Volume 148

Series Editor

Lisa Firth

Independence

Educational Publishers
Cambridge

First published by Independence
The Studio, High Green
Great Shelford
Cambridge CB22 5EG
England

© Independence 2008

British Library Cataloguing in Publication Data
Religious Beliefs – (Issues Series)
I. Firth, Lisa II. Series
200.9'41

ISBN 978 1 86168 421 9

Printed in Great Britain
MWL Print Group Ltd

Cover
The illustration on the front cover is by
Don Hatcher.

CONTENTS

Useful information for readers

Dear Reader,

Issues: Religious Beliefs

Britain today is a diverse society, and the various religions practised in the UK reflect this. Christianity is the state religion and also the most popular in the UK, with census data showing that 72% of people claim to be Christians. However, only 7% of the population attend church regularly and this figure continues to fall. Meanwhile, Islam is now Britain's second most popular religion, accounting for 3% of the population according to the census. This book covers issues such as religious diversity, tolerance and discrimination, religious extremism, values and ethics and the controversy surrounding religion in education.

The purpose of *Issues*

Religious Beliefs is the one hundred and forty-eighth volume in the **Issues** series. The aim of this series is to offer up-to-date information about important issues in our world. Whether you are a regular reader or new to the series, we do hope you find this book a useful overview of the many and complex issues involved in the topic.

Titles in the **Issues** series are resource books designed to be of especial use to those undertaking project work or requiring an overview of facts, opinions and information on a particular subject, particularly as a prelude to undertaking their own research.

The information in this book is not from a single author, publication or organisation; the value of this unique series lies in the fact that it presents information from a wide variety of sources, including:
⇨ Government reports and statistics
⇨ Newspaper articles and features
⇨ Information from think-tanks and policy institutes
⇨ Magazine features and surveys
⇨ Website material
⇨ Literature from lobby groups and charitable organisations.*

Critical evaluation

Because the information reprinted here is from a number of different sources, readers should bear in mind the origin of the text and whether the source is likely to have a particular bias or agenda when presenting information (just as they would if undertaking their own research). It is hoped that, as you read about the many aspects of the issues explored in this book, you will critically evaluate the information presented. It is important that you decide whether you are being presented with facts or opinions. Does the writer give a biased or an unbiased report? If an opinion is being expressed, do you agree with the writer?

Religious Beliefs offers a useful starting point for those who need convenient access to information about the many issues involved. However, it is only a starting point. Following each article is a URL to the relevant organisation's website, which you may wish to visit for further information.

Kind regards,

Lisa Firth
Editor, **Issues** series

** Please note that Independence Publishers has no political affiliations or opinions on the topics covered in the **Issues** series, and any views quoted in this book are not necessarily those of the publisher or its staff.*

What is religion?

God, ethics, community or what? Information from Channel 4

Similar ideas underpin many of the religions found in the world, although they may be expressed in very different ways. The word 'religion' comes from the Latin *religio*, which means 'duty', and religions often impose rules on their followers.

Spirituality

A vital part of many religions is belief in the individual's spirit or soul as an entity which is distinct from the body and mind. This spirit is immortal and, after physical death, continues its existence in an invisible spiritual world, where it may be punished or rewarded for deeds performed during life. Followers of a religion often lead their lives in a prescribed way in order to be allowed to enter the spiritual realm after death.

Another key concept in most religions is belief in one or more higher beings who, as creators of the universe, have power over nature and the lives of people. These beings are often worshipped, and may be named deities or seen as unimaginable sources of absolute power.

Many religions offer their followers answers to philosophical questions about topics such as how and why the universe came into existence, the purpose of life and the best way to live it, and what happens after death.

Worship and ritual

Worship and prayer often take place during ceremonies or rituals. Worshippers may gather at a temple, church or other sacred place, and may kneel or stand, cover their heads, or wash their feet before praying. Items such as beads, candles, fire or bells help to focus concentration.

Prayer can be spoken, chanted or sung out loud, or may be expressed silently. It is used as a way of offering praise and thanks, asking for mediation, confirming continued faith, or meditating on the divine. Most religions have festivals to celebrate events such as the anniversary of the birth or death of a leader or prophet, or a seasonal event on which the community depends, such as harvest or sowing.

Sacred places range from vast, lavishly decorated and opulent cathedrals to small, plain shrines in the open air. Some places attract pilgrims because of their longstanding religious associations, for instance as the site of a martyrdom or holy event.

Similar ideas underpin many of the religions found in the world

---

Sources of authority

Religious texts or scriptures often form a part of worship and are treated with great respect. In some religions they are thought to be the unchanging word of god, while in others they are seen as emanating from god via a human channel, and as being open to changing interpretations.

The official ministers of a religion usually have a range of duties. They may lead acts of worship and endeavour to guide followers into patterns of steadfast belief. There are usually strict rules about who may become a priest, and women are often excluded from the priesthood. Monks and nuns or their equivalents dedicate their lives to a religion, usually leading a simple and celibate life away from mainstream society, and dedicating themselves to prayer, study, meditation and, sometimes, charitable work.

What is it for?

Religion has many functions in people's lives. It can provide an explanation for the numerous inexplicable phenomena in the world, including natural events and human suffering. Religion provides an ethical framework for its followers' lives, and can be a source of great solace and comfort. Faith can allay fear, even in the face of extreme suffering or death.

Shared religious belief binds families together, and consolidates communities and countries, although conflict over religious matters can cause rifts and even wars. When passed down through generations, religious beliefs bring continuity, while ceremonies are important rites of passage, marking out people's lives from birth, through coming of age, to marriage and eventually death.

Religion has been, and in many places continues to be, used as a means of imposing control on society and individuals. It does this by establishing rules which dictate definitions of acceptable behaviour, control the free expression of sexuality, and prescribe the place of men and women in both the family and in wider society.

If there's no god

Although worldwide religious following is increasing, many people do not include religion in their lives. Atheists believe that there is no god, while agnostics are unsure whether a god exists or not. Humanists think that it is possible to achieve happiness and fulfilment through human behaviour alone, and secularists argue that religion should not play any part in the political or educational systems of a country.

⇨ This extract is from the Channel 4 Faith and Belief website at www.channel4.com/belief and is reprinted with kind permission.

© Channel 4

Major religions in the UK

Information from the University of Manchester

Buddhism

Buddhism is more than 2,500 years old and has more than 2,000 sects. It developed in North India in the 6th or 5th century BC, when Siddhartha Gautama attained 'enlightenment' – the ultimate truth by which people are freed from the cycle of re-birth.

Buddhists do not worship gods or deities. Buddhists believe that the pathway to enlightenment is found by personal spiritual development. Buddhism developed from Hinduism, and while there are some fundamental differences between the two there are also some core beliefs which they both share.

> **There are over 1 billion Christians in the world today, making it the world's largest religion**

There are approximately 350 million Buddhists worldwide with the 2001 Census suggesting that there are approximately 152,000 Buddhists living in Britain today.

Festivals

Because of the wide variety of Buddhism in the world it is impossible to represent all of the denominations and varying traditions, although they would include:

⇨ Nirvana Day – Celebrated on 15 February, it is the date that Buddhists observe his passing.
⇨ Buddha Day – This is the celebration of the Buddha's birth. It occurs on 8 April.
⇨ Bodhi Day – This day marks the day that Siddhartha sat under the tree (a Bodhi tree) and eventually attained or enlightened.

Dietary requirements

Buddhists advocate vegetarianism but it is not obligatory.

Dress code

There are no religious laws governing specific dress code.

Christianity

There are over 1 billion Christians in the world today, making it the world's largest religion.

Christianity originated in the Middle East and is now over 2,000 years old. Christians believe in one God and that God revealed himself to mankind as Father, Son and Holy Spirit.

It is also believed that he has revealed Himself through the Bible and through his Son, Jesus Christ.

Christianity is divided into four principal denominations: Orthodox, Pentecostal, Protestant and Roman Catholic. However, all Christians believe that Jesus of Nazareth is the Son of God who lived on earth as a human being, was crucified as part of God's plan for redeeming the sins of mankind, and then rose from the dead. For Christians, Jesus is the saviour of the human race.

Holy Communion – also referred to as the Mass, the Eucharist and the Lord's Supper – is a pivotal aspect of Christian worship. Worshippers consume bread and wine as a token of the body and blood of Christ sacrificed for human sins.

The Christian in the workplace

The standard working week and public holidays have been influenced by the traditions and religious observances of Christianity.

Festivals

Different forms of Christianity celebrate different festivals and observe different holy days, but all forms observe (though might not celebrate in the same way) the following six holy days:

⇨ Christmas – 25 December. Marks the birth of Jesus Christ.
⇨ Good Friday – The Friday before Easter (March/April, time varies), it commemorates Jesus' passion (suffering) on the cross.
⇨ Easter – Marks the resurrection of Jesus from the tomb.
⇨ Ascension – Forty days after Easter, the ascension of Christ to heaven is commemorated.
⇨ Pentecost – The seventh Sunday after Easter. Marks the decent of the Holy Spirit upon the apostles, which began the work of the Church.

Dietary requirements

Christian dietary habits tend to be culturally rather than religiously determined. However, some African and South Asian Christians may avoid pork. Alcohol is forbidden according to some Christian groups, although drinking wine (in moderation) plays a symbolic role in Holy Communion.

Dress code

There are no religious laws governing dress code. Christians will wear clothes according to their cultural or national origin. As a result, it would not be out of the ordinary to see a South Asian Christian woman wearing a shalwar kameez or sari. Some conservative European Christians ascertain that women must wear hats in church.

Bereavement

No special requirement beyond normal compassionate leave.

Hinduism

The term 'Hinduism' is used to describe the ancient religious culture of India. This culture is over 5,000 years old and is practised by countless millions.

Hinduism has neither a single founder, nor a single scripture that is uniquely authoritative.

Hinduism is an amalgamation of several faith traditions. It may be helpful to view Hinduism not so much as a single religion, but as a family of religions. Hindus themselves use various terms such as sanatana-dharma (loosely translated as 'eternal religion') to describe their faith; the word 'Hindu' is originally a geographic designation (those who live east of the Indus River) and is not found in any Hindu scriptures.

With 400,000 followers, Hinduism is the fourth largest religion in the UK.

Hindus support fully the notion of reincarnation and that behaviour in this life determines your moral status in the next. There is also a caste system which was introduced by the supreme deity, Brahman. This system is intended to create a just but hierarchical society in which different groups have different hereditary rights.

Hindu worship is a private matter for each individual. A devout Hindu will usually worship in their home in a room specifically set aside for this purpose. They will also celebrate, along with their community, many religious and cultural festivals.

Diwali is the Hindu festival of lights

Festivals

Hindu holy days and festivals follow a lunar calendar, thus dates vary from year to year. A few of the most popular are:

⇨ Diwali – Known as the festival of lights, this commemorates the return of Lord Rama from his exile in the forest. It is, for many traditions, a new-year celebration. It takes place between late October and the middle of November.

⇨ Dussehra – A celebration of good conquering evil, this festival lasts ten days and takes place between late September and the middle of October.

⇨ Holi – A spring festival to celebrate creation and renewal, linked with Lord Krishna.

⇨ Navaratri – A nine-day festival which celebrates the triumph of good over evil.

⇨ Janmastami – A celebration marking the appearance on earth of Lord Krishna.

Dietary requirements

Hindus uphold the sacredness of all life, including animal life. Devout Hindus will neither eat meat nor fish. Some will not eat eggs. Even those Hindus who have decided to eat meat will nonetheless refuse to eat beef since the cow is seen as a sacred animal. Hinduism forbids the consumption of alcohol. Garlic and onions are thought to be foods discarded by the gods. Strictly orthodox Hindus will not eat food prepared by someone not belonging to the same level of caste as them.

Hindus don't observe any specific cultural dress with stringency. They will gladly wear clothes from other countries, including Western attire. However, Hindu men typically wear a pyjama (narrow trousers) and kurta, which is a loose fitting shirt. Women often wear a sari, a long piece of material wrapped around the body. Married Hindu women wear a bindi – a red powder spot marked on the forehead.

Bereavement

Following cremation, close relatives of the deceased will observe a 13-day mourning period during which they will wish to remain at home. The closest male relatives may take the ashes of the deceased to the Ganges, in India. They may therefore request extended leave. Close male relatives of the deceased may shave their heads as a mark of respect.

Islam

There are over a thousand million Muslims (people who follow Islam) in the world today. The word 'Islam' literally means 'submission' (to God). This monotheistic religion was founded by the Prophet Muhammad over 1,300 years ago.

There are roughly 2.5-3 million Muslims living in Britain today, which makes it the 2nd most popular religion in the UK.

Muslims believe that there is only one God, Allah, and that the Prophet Muhammad (Peace Be Upon Him) was his final messenger. The Quran and Sunnah together provide authoritative source for Muslim law (Shariah).

Muslims must witness publicly to the unity of God and the prophethood of Muhammad. This is the first pillar of faith. The remaining compulsory faiths are: five scheduled daily prayers, fasting in the holy month of Ramadan, payment of the alms tax annually and the Hajj, a pilgrimage to Mecca, once in a lifetime (finances permitting).

Muslims celebrate several religious festivals. The Eid ul-Fitr celebrates the end of the month of abstinence observed in Ramadhan.

There are roughly 2.5-3 million Muslims living in Britain today, which makes it the 2nd most popular religion in the UK

The Eid ul-Adha, celebrated approximately 70 days after Eid ul-Fitr, is centred around the sacrificing of animals and the distribution of meat to the needy.

Festivals

⇨ Ramadan – This Holy Festival takes place in the ninth month of the Islamic calendar. It is a time of fasting and daily repentance.

⇨ Lailut ul-Qadr – The final 10 days of Ramadan. Muslims celebrate Muhammad's first revelation.

⇨ Eid ul-Fitr – The feast period just after the month-long fast of Ramadan. It lasts for three days.

⇨ Eid ul-Adha – Two to three months after Ramadan, animals are slaughtered to benefit the poor. The purpose of the Eid ul-Adha is to celebrate the faithfulness and obedience of Abraham.

⇨ Al-Isra Wal Miraj – Day of the 17th month in the Islamic calendar. It marks Muhammad's journey from Mecca.

⇨ Maulid al-Nabi – Celebrates the birth of Muhammad.

Dietary requirements

In Islam, all food is classified as either halal (lawful) or haram (prohibited). Religious law requires that animals be slaughtered by a trained person in the name of God. An animal should not be stunned before slaughter; a quick deep stroke of a sharp knife across the throat is required. Pork and alcohol are absolutely forbidden.

It should be made clear that utensils used to serve haram food cannot be used on halal food.

Dress code

Both men and women are required to dress and behave modestly. Once a young woman reaches puberty, she must cover her hair and wear loose flowing opaque garments, which conceal the shape of her body. This style of dress (hijab) must be practised in the presence of all men except those with whom a woman is forbidden to marry, such as her father or brothers. Men should dress modestly. Western clothes may be worn as long as they fulfil the criterion of modesty.

Bereavement

Burial must take place as soon as possible following death and may therefore occur at short notice.

Other

⇨ Any form of gambling is forbidden under Islam.
⇨ Observant Muslims are required to wash following use of the toilet and will therefore appreciate access to water in the toilet cubicle, often Muslims will carry a small container of water into the cubicle for this purpose. By agreement with other staff and cleaners, these containers could be kept in the cubicle.
⇨ Physical contact between the sexes is discouraged and some Muslims may politely refuse to shake hands with the opposite sex. This should not be viewed negatively.

Judaism

There are approximately 12 million Jews in the world today.

Judaism originated in the Middle East and is based on the belief in one God. According to Torah, the central scripture for Jews, God is holy and unmitigated. He is omnipotent, omniscient and eternal. The rules and traditions an observant Jew follows are known collectively as the halakha (the path).

According to Orthodox Judaism, 613 commandments (or mitzvoth) lie at the heart of the halakha. God in

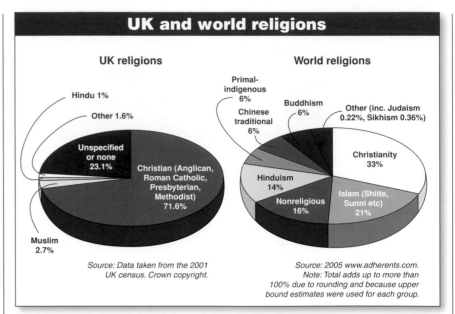

the Torah gave some of these, while others were added by the rabbis and derived from ancient Jewish customs. Apart from the written Torah, there is a verbal Torah that is an attempt to understand and apply the written version.

Festivals

Jews celebrate many religious and cultural festivals associated with significant historical events in Jewish history. The Passover commemorates the Israelites' deliverance from slavery in Egypt. Rosh Hashana is the Jewish New Year. It coincides with beginning of the Ten Days of Repentance. The last of these days is the Day of Atonement (Yom Kippur), the holiest day in the Jewish calendar. The Sabbath (Shabbat) is a day of complete rest and starts on Friday immediately before dusk and ends after dusk on Saturday. Therefore a practising Jew must be able to leave work in sufficient time to arrive home by the start of the Sabbath.

⇨ Rosh Hashana – The Jewish New Year. Occurs around the middle of September/October. It celebrates the religious New Year and the creation of earth.
⇨ Yom Kippur – Occurs shortly after Rosh Hashana. It is the Day of Atonement. It runs from sunset to sunset and believers do not eat or drink during this time. It is a time to repent for actions of the past year.
⇨ Sukkot – The feast of Booths. It last for eight days and occurs around the end of October. It is known as the Harvest celebration.

⇨ Channukah (Hannukkah) – Occurs early to mid December. Known as the Festival of Lights it celebrates the victory of the Maccabees over the Syrians in the second century BCE.
⇨ Purim – Occurs late February to early March. It remembers the deliverance of the Persian Jews from destruction. The day before Purim is spent fasting, the actual day of Purim is joyous.
⇨ Pesach (Passover) – Occurs from late March to early April. It honours the delivery of the Jewish people from slavery. It lasts between 7 and 8 days (depending on the branch of Judaism).
⇨ Shavout – Occurs in May/June and lasts for 2 days. It is the spring harvest festival and the celebration of God's gift of the Torah.

Dietary requirements

Jews are religiously obliged to eat kosher food. That is to say that a devout Jew can only eat certain types of meat and fish. Meat must be prepared in a ritually acceptable manner. Meat and dairy products must not be eaten in the same meal. Pork is forbidden to Jews.

Dress code

It is imperative that practising Jewish men keep their head covered at all times generally by wearing a Kippah (skull cap). Orthodox Jewish women are required to dress modestly.

Bereavement

Funerals must take place as soon as possible following the death – the same day where possible – and therefore take place at short notice. Following a death, the immediate family must stay at home and mourn for seven days (Shiva). Following the death of a father or mother, an observant Jewish man will be required to go to a synagogue to pray morning, afternoon and evening for 11 months of the Jewish calendar.

Sikhism

Sikhism is a monotheistic faith, which was founded in the fifteenth century by Guru Nanak in the region of Punjab, north-west India. It is recognised as the youngest of world religions.

Sikhism emerged as a result of the teachings of Guru Nanak whose aim was to encourage all people to faithfully worship one God. The fundamentals of the religion were then further developed by a continuous line of nine gurus (teachers) who succeeded him.

The last guru declared that after him, there would be no other gurus. The Guru Granth Sahib, the Sikh holy book, would be viewed as the eternal guru. For Sikhs the Granth Sahib is the focal point of a Sikh temple (Gurdwara) and the ultimate source of religious authority.

Festivals
Sikhs celebrate several religious festivals that combine a cultural and religious significance.
⇨ Vaisakhi – the central festival which is a dual celebration incorporating both a harvest festival and a commemoration of Guru Gobind Singh's creation of the Khalsa, the pure brotherhood of Sikhs.
⇨ Diwali – Known as the festival of lights, this commemorates the return of Lord Rama from his exile in the forest. It is, for many traditions, a new-year celebration. It takes place between late October and the middle of November.
⇨ Gurpurbs – The marking of important anniversaries relating to the birth or death (martyrdom) of a Guru. This includes the full recitation of the Guru Granth Sahib as well as the singing of hymns and Sikh lectures.

Sikhism is recognised as the youngest of world religions

⇨ Baisakhi – The day is celebrated around 13 April. It is the celebration of the founding of the Khalsa Order and Sikh nation. Many Sikhs choose to be initiated on this day. Often, a religious street procession marks the key event.
⇨ Bandi Chhor – Sikhs commemorate the release of Guru Hargobind (Sixth Guru) from false imprisonment. It coincides with the Indian Festival of Lights (Diwali) between the end of October and mid-November. A Muslim saint laid the foundation stone of the Golden Temple, also on this day.
⇨ Maghi – This celebration occurs around the middle of January and marks the martyrdom of forty Sikhs at the hands of the Mughal army.
⇨ Hola Mohalla – On this day Sikhs practise military exercises, stage mock battles, perform martial arts and organise sports competitions. This is to keep the martial skills and spirit alive. Hymn singing and lectures also take place. It occurs the day after the Indian festival Holi around mid-March.

Dietary requirements
Sikhism forbids smoking and the consumption of alcohol. A devout Sikh will neither eat eggs, nor any animal by-product. Many Sikhs do not eat meat either. Sikhs regard the cow as a sacred animal and the pig is thought to be dirty – hence the prohibition of pork.

Sikh men are religiously required to wear turbans to cover their uncut hair. Should she choose, a Sikh woman may also wear a turban. Young Sikh boys will wear their long hair tied in a topknot. The five Ks will be worn on the person: some will be visible, such as the Kesh (uncut hair covered by a turban) and Kara (steel bracelet), while others, such as the Kirpan (sword) and Katcha (shorts) will be worn under the clothes. Some married women, like their Hindu counterparts, may also wear a Bindi – a red powder spot marked on the forehead.

Bereavement
Sikhs are cremated and have a preference for this to take place as soon after the death as possible. There is no specified mourning period and normal compassionate leave arrangements should suffice.

⇨ The above information is taken from the website of the University of Manchester and is reprinted with their consent. Visit www.manchester.ac.uk for more information.
© University of Manchester

Religion in Britain, and in the rest of the UK

Information from Religious Tolerance

'[Religion] as George Carey so dramatically put it in 1998, is "bleeding to death." Although many Britons would claim to be "C of E", it seems the allegiance stretches only as far as "hatches, matches and dispatches" – being baptised, married and buried in Anglican ceremonies.' Brian Draper, in an Amazon.co.uk book review.
'…people questioned about how much they go to church, give figures which, if true, would add up to twice those given by the churches.' Monica Furlong.
'Organised religion is in near-terminal decline in Britain…' Matt Barnwell & Amy Iggulden, of the Telegraph.
'…the British are now a largely irreligious people. Only a minority believe that God exists and almost everyone acknowledges that Britain is becoming an increasingly secular society.' Anthony King, The Telegraph.

Importance of religion

The Institute for Social Research at the University of Michigan periodically conducts the World Values Survey. It polls a statistically valid sample of adults from a total of 60 nations. In their 1995-1997 survey, they found that:

⇨ 16% of the British adult population consider religion to be very important in their lives.
⇨ 53% in the US,
⇨ 14% in France, and
⇨ 13% in Germany agreed.

The Pew Research Center conducted a more recent series of studies called 'The Pew Global Attitudes Project'. They are measuring the 'impact of globalisation, modernisation, rapid technological and cultural change and the Sept. 11 terrorist events on the values and attitudes of more than 38,000 people in 44 countries...' A poll released on 19 December 2002 revealed whether people around the world consider religion to be personally important.

Results showed that the percentage of the public who considered religion important ranged from 97% in Senegal to 11% in both France and the Czech Republic in the 41 countries sampled. They found that the percentage was:

⇨ 59% in the United States;
⇨ 57% in Mexico;
⇨ 33% in Great Britain;
⇨ 30% in Canada.

Information on other countries

The disparity between the World Values Survey's 16% and the Pew Global Attitude Project's 33% may be an accurate representation of a real increase in interest over a four- or five-year interval, from about 1997 to 2002. However, it is more likely due to a difference in the specific question asked. On matters of religion, people tend to give the answer that is expected of them, rather than the truth. So, results often differ because of the setting, the nature of the questioning, and the specific question asked.

Christian denominations

Data from 1992 show that only 14.4% of the UK population belong to a Christian denomination. The vast majority of Christian church members are affiliated with the Roman Catholic Church, the Church of England, or the Presbyterian Church:

Denomination and number of members (million)

⇨ Roman Catholic: 2.044
⇨ Church of England: 1.808
⇨ Presbyterian: 1.242
⇨ Methodist: 0.459
⇨ Independent: 0.357
⇨ Eastern Orthodox: 0.276
⇨ Baptist: 0.231
⇨ Pentecostal: 0.170
⇨ Other: 0.131

Numbers of followers

On 14 February 2003, TimesOnline published the results from the 29 April 2001 decennial government census. For the first time since 1851, the census included a question on religion. It was the only optional question on the census. Over 92% of the population answered it.

The results indicate that Britain remains a Christian country, at least in terms of religious affiliation. In the 29 April 2001 census, out of a total population of 58.79 million:

Religion, number (in millions and as percentage of total population)

⇨ Christianity: 42.079 (71.6%)
⇨ No religion (Incl. Jedi): 9.10 (15.5%)
⇨ Refused to answer: 4.29 (7.3%)
⇨ Islam: 1.59 (2.7%)
⇨ Hinduism: 0.559 (1.0%)
⇨ Sikhism: 0.336 (0.6%)
⇨ Judaism: 0.267 (0.5%)
⇨ Buddhism: 0.152 (0.3%)
⇨ Other: 0.179 (0.3%)
⇨ **Total population: 58.789 (100.0%)**

Reaction to the Times Online poll

'Jedism' appears to be the fourth most popular religion in the UK, with 390,000 adults (0.66% of the population) identifying themselves as followers of this religion. This refers to the spirituality expressed by the characters in Star Wars. These are the 'May the force be with you' folks. Very few subjects who marked this 'religion' during the poll are actually Jedi. They probably intended their vote to be a statement about their opinion of religion, religious polls, or the government census. A hoax e-mail circulated around the Internet stating that if 10,000 people put 'Jedi' on the census form, it will become 'a fully recognised and legal religion'. The Office of National Statistics assigned the response 'Jedi Knight' a numeric code to simplify the process of tabulating census results, as is typically done when many people answer a question by writing in a response not offered as a choice on the census form. Since the government does not recognise Jedism as an actual religion, the Jedis were finally lumped together under the 'no religion' category.

Graham Zellick, vice chancellor of the University of London, opposed the religious question, and urged that people refuse to answer the question. He said: 'It is improper to use the unique power of the State to ascertain information so that these bodies can carry out their own functions. It is wholly inconsistent with our traditions of freedom and personal privacy to ask a question about a person's religious beliefs.'

The Right Rev Keith Sutton, the Bishop of Lichfield, said: 'These figures prove as a lie claims that England is no longer a Christian country. Clergy in my diocese baptise some 23 per cent of all babies before they are one year old. The Christian faith is still relevant to many, many people... But welcome as they are, the statistics are a wake-up call to all of us in Christian leadership. While the Christian faith remains relevant to the vast majority of society, the Church is clearly no longer seen as important.'

Iqbal Sacranie, secretary-general of the Muslim Council of Britain, said: 'Up to now, Muslims have been statistically invisible, and thus easily marginalised. The census output is a strong signal to central and local government, social services and employers in particular that the needs of all sections of Britain's multicultural society must be fairly and equitably addressed.'

Professors Barry Kosmin and Stanley Waterman, of the Institute for Jewish Policy Research, suggested that the total of Jews had been undercounted. 'Nationally, 15.5 per cent of the population stated that they had no religion and 7.3 per cent did not answer the question. In other words, almost a quarter of the population did not provide a specific religious preference...This alone suggests that the number of Jews is undercounted. This was not unexpected and, in fact, there are grounds for suggesting that Jews may be more reluctant than others to answer a voluntary question on religion in the census. For historical reasons, many older Jews of Central and Eastern European background are reluctant to cooperate with government-sponsored counts of Jews.'

'Organised religion is in near-terminal decline in Britain'

The followers of some religions are reluctant to admit their identification. Vexen Crabtree wrote that: '... at a London Satanists gathering I polled all the members present about what they had put on the 2001 April National Census, and half of them said they had put "no religion". This is a significant under-representation.' Wiccans and other Neopagans are probably under-represented as well.

Degree of commitment
During the 2001 poll, 72% identified themselves as 'Christian'. This does not necessarily indicate that they are committed Christians. Vexen Crabtree collected some statistics from a variety of sources which indicate that many of these folks are Christian in name only:

The Office of National Statistics found in the 2001 census that: '...half of all adults aged 18 and over who belonged to a religion have never attended a religious service.'

Uk.news.yahoo.com reported in 2000 that '[Church attendance in 1999 was] 7.5% on an average Sunday, [down] from 10% in 1989 and 12% in 1979.'

A New Scientist Poll in Autumn 2002 showed that '55% of British public do not believe in a higher being.'

A 2004 government report revealed that about 74% of adults in England and Wales regard themselves as Christians. Another approximately 6% identify with another religion. But only about 7% of Christians in the UK actually attend church regularly. Hanne Stinson, director of the British Humanist Association, said that many adults are 'cultural Christians'. They see themselves as being Christian in the same way that they are British, almost in a tribal way. She said: 'People label themselves with what they were brought up with...If they haven't gone to church for 20 years, they still put themselves down on official forms as "Church of England".'

Recent trends
After reviewing a report by the University of Manchester in August 2005, News.Telegraph reported that 'Organised religion is in near-terminal decline in Britain because parents have only a 50-50 chance of passing on belief to their offspring.' Dr David Voas, who oversaw the study, said that religion would reach 'fairly low levels [before very long]. The dip in religious belief is not temporary or accidental, it is a generational phenomenon – the decline has continued year on year. The fact that children are only half as likely to believe as their parents indicates that, as a society, we are at an advanced stage of secularisation.'

Their report was based on interviews of 10,500 households over 14 years and used data from the British Household Panel and British Social Attitudes surveys. They found that between 1991 and 1999:
⇨ The importance of belief in God fell from 37.8% to 32.5%;
⇨ The percentage of people who attended church services fell by 3.5%;
⇨ The percentage of people who regard themselves as affiliated with a religion dropped by 2.9%.

There was diverse reaction to the survey results:

Steve Jenkins, a spokesperson for the Church of England, was sceptical. He said: 'There is an assumption that people "catch" religion from their parents, but many people come to faith through the grandparents, schools, and their friends.' He said that the study had not released 'proper evidence...There is nothing to back up the claims. Our recent statistics show that congregations are actually increasing, as is the number of ordinations.' Church of England data show that in 2004, the ordinations of 564 people were approved – the highest figure in six years. Congregations in 2003 had increased in size by 1 per cent.

This compares to a total population growth which averages about 0.3% a year.

The National Secular Society welcomed the results. Their vice president, Terry Sanderson, said: 'We find [belief] embarrassing as a country and it is time we accepted that...People may say they believe in Christianity but if you question them even slightly it becomes clear that they cannot accept the central tenets of its faith – they don't believe in its supernatural explanations.'

Results of the December 2004 YouGov survey

According to the *Telegraph*:

'...a YouGov survey provides overwhelming evidence that the British are now a largely irreligious people. Only a minority believe that God exists and almost everyone acknowledges that Britain is becoming an increasingly secular society...the national mood appears to be one of benign indifference.'

YouGov polled 1,981 adults across Britain during 16 to 18 December 2004. The margin of error was about ±>2.5 percentage points. Some results:

⇨ A minority, 44%, believe in God. This is a drop from 77% in 1968 – an unusually rapid change for religious matters.
⇨ Of those who believe in God, 3% believe in more than one God and 10% believe in 'some other kind of Supreme Being'.
⇨ 33% believe in the existence of Heaven.
⇨ 25% believe in Hell. This result has changed little since 1968.
⇨ Over a third of young adults describe themselves as Agnostic or Atheist.

Results of the May 2005 MORI poll

This survey polled 4,270 adults. The margin of error would have been less than ±>2 percentage points. Some results:

⇨ 36% of young adults (18 to 34 years of age) define themselves as Atheist or Agnostic.
⇨ 24% of the adult population as a whole say they have no religion.
⇨ 11% of those over 65 say they have no religion. The non-religious figure falls to 11%.

⇨ The above information is re-printed with kind permission from Religious Tolerance. Visit www.religioustolerance.org for more information or to view notes and references.

© Religious Tolerance

The Golden Rule

A humanist discussion

All societies and religions have moral principles, laws and rules. Although many of the less important rules vary, all traditions seem to have come up with a version of 'the Golden Rule', 'Do as you would be done by' or 'Treat other people in a way you would like to be treated yourself' – there are more examples below. It can be expressed positively (as above) or negatively ('Do not treat others as you would not like to be treated yourself'). Some people think that the negative versions are better, because it is easier to agree on the things we would not like, and anyone can work out what would cause suffering to themselves or another person and then avoid doing it. For example, you wouldn't want to be bullied, so you shouldn't bully other people.

The Golden Rule requires kindness and care for the less fortunate, because this is what we would want in their situation, and it discourages actions like lying and theft because no one wants to be lied to or to have their property stolen. It is simple and clear, and works well in practice.

Humanists seek to live good lives without religious or superstitious beliefs. They use reason, experience and respect for others when thinking about moral issues, not obedience to dogmatic rules. They are impressed by the fact that we find this very useful basic principle everywhere. It appears to be based on our common humanity, using our need to be treated well by others and our aspiration to live harmoniously with others as its foundation. It can be worked out by anyone, anywhere, by thinking about our understanding of ourselves and other people. It does not need to be given to us by sacred texts or a god.

Questions to think about

⇨ Write out each version of the Golden Rule on a map of the world and draw a line to the place each one comes from.
⇨ Why do you think so many different cultures have come up with something so similar?
⇨ Do you think the Golden Rule is enough on its own?
⇨ Would it stop people lying or stealing or killing people?
⇨ If people followed it, would they always do the right thing?

⇨ If they disobeyed it, would they tend to do bad things?
⇨ Would the world be a better place if everyone, including world leaders, obeyed the Golden Rule?
⇨ What are rules for?
⇨ Think about your family rules. (They may not be written down but most families have some 'rules' – like 'Everybody makes their own bed'.) What are they for? Are they based on the Golden Rule?
⇨ Think about school rules – what are they for? Are any of them based on the Golden Rule?
⇨ What are good manners for? Are they anything to do with the Golden Rule?
⇨ If you were only allowed one school rule, what would you choose?
⇨ What should you do when people break the Golden Rule?
⇨ If you ruled the world for a day, what rule or rules would you establish to make the world a better place?

Examples of the Golden Rule from around the world

'He should treat all beings as he himself should be treated. The essence of right conduct is not to injure anyone.' (JAINISM – from The Suta-Kritanga, about 550 BCE*)

'Do not do to others what you would not like for yourself.' (CONFUCIANISM – from The Analects of Confucius, about 500 BCE)

'I will act towards others exactly as I would act towards myself.' (BUDDHISM – from The Siglo-Vada Sutta, about 500 BCE)

'This is the sum of duty: Do nothing to others which, if done to you, could cause you pain.' (HINDUISM – from The Mahabharata, about 150 BCE)

'What you would avoid suffering yourself, seek not to impose on others.' (ANCIENT GREECE – Epictetus, the Greek philosopher, about 90 CE*)

'Love your neighbour as yourself.' (JUDAISM / CHRISTIANITY – Leviticus 19, in The Torah, about

400 BCE, quoted by Jesus in Matthew 22 and Mark 12, 1st century CE)

'What is harmful to yourself do not do to your fellow men. That is the whole of the law...' (JUDAISM – from Hillel: The Talmud, about 100 CE)

'None of you truly believes, until he wishes for his brothers what he wishes for himself.' (ISLAM – a saying of the Prophet Muhammad, 7th century CE)

'As you think of yourself, so think of others.' (SIKHISM – from Guru Granth Sahib, 1604 CE)

One should be 'contented with so much liberty against other men, as he would allow against himself.' (GREAT BRITAIN – Thomas Hobbes, English philosopher, 1588-1679 CE)

'He should not wish for others what he does not wish for himself.' (BAHA'I from the writings of Baha'u'llah, about 1870 CE)

'You should always ask yourself what would happen if everyone did what you are doing.' (FRANCE – Jean-Paul Sartre, French existentialist philosopher, 1905-80 CE)

'Treat other people as you'd want to be treated in their situation; don't do things you wouldn't want to have done to you.' (British Humanist Association, 1999 CE)

* BCE = Before Common Era, equivalent to BC.
CE = Common Era, equivalent to AD.
Updated February 2006

⇨ The above information is re-printed with kind permission from the British Humanist Association. For more information on this and other related issues, please visit www.humanism.org.uk

© British Humanist Association

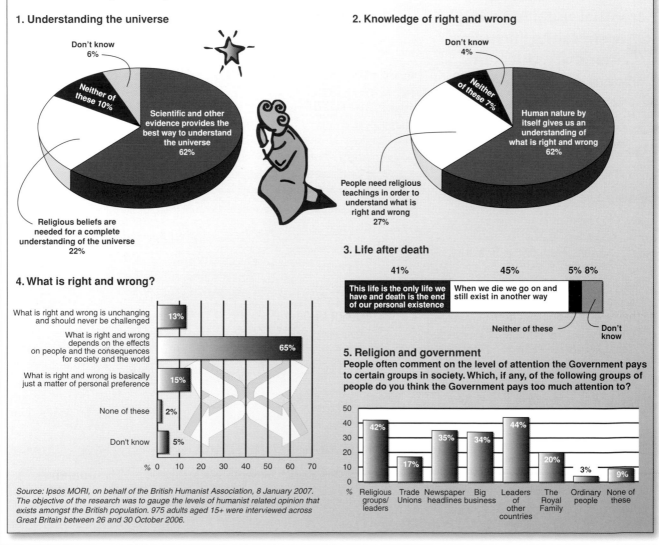

Religious and humanist beliefs in Britain

For questions 1-4, respondents were told: 'I am going to read out some pairs of statements to you. I'd like you to tell me on balance which one in each pair most closely matches your view. You might find that the statements overlap a little, however please tell me which one you feel most closely matches your view. (If you had to choose just one of the statements which one best matches your view?)'

1. Understanding the universe

Don't know 6%
Neither of these 10%
Scientific and other evidence provides the best way to understand the universe 62%
Religious beliefs are needed for a complete understanding of the universe 22%

2. Knowledge of right and wrong

Don't know 4%
Neither of these 7%
Human nature by itself gives us an understanding of what is right and wrong 62%
People need religious teachings in order to understand what is right and wrong 27%

3. Life after death

| 41% | 45% | 5% | 8% |
| This life is the only life we have and death is the end of our personal existence | When we die we go on and still exist in another way | Neither of these | Don't know |

4. What is right and wrong?

What is right and wrong is unchanging and should never be challenged — 13%
What is right and wrong depends on the effects on people and the consequences for society and the world — 65%
What is right and wrong is basically just a matter of personal preference — 15%
None of these — 2%
Don't know — 5%

% 0 10 20 30 40 50 60 70

5. Religion and government

People often comment on the level of attention the Government pays to certain groups in society. Which, if any, of the following groups of people do you think the Government pays too much attention to?

| Religious groups/leaders | Trade Unions | Newspaper headlines | Big business | Leaders of other countries | The Royal Family | Ordinary people | None of these |
| 42% | 17% | 35% | 34% | 44% | 20% | 3% | 9% |

Source: Ipsos MORI, on behalf of the British Humanist Association, 8 January 2007. The objective of the research was to gauge the levels of humanist related opinion that exists amongst the British population. 975 adults aged 15+ were interviewed across Great Britain between 26 and 30 October 2006.

Food culture and religion

Information from the Better Health Channel

Food is an important part of religious observance and spiritual ritual for many different faiths, including Christianity, Judaism, Islam, Hinduism and Buddhism. The role of food in cultural practices and religious beliefs is complex and varies among individuals and communities. The following article is not all-encompassing. It is an introduction to a diverse and complex topic, and includes some of the ways in which various religious groups include food as a vital part of their faith.

Food is an important part of religious observance and spiritual ritual for many different faiths, including Christianity, Judaism, Islam, Hinduism and Buddhism

---

Christianity

The various faiths of Christianity include Roman Catholic, Orthodox and Protestant. The regulations governing food differ from one to the next, including some faiths that don't advocate any restrictions. Selected facts include:

⇨ The ritual of the transubstantiation (changing) of bread and wine into the body and blood of Jesus Christ is believed to occur at communion.

⇨ Roman Catholics fast for at least one hour prior to communion.

⇨ Fasting is sometimes considered to be 'praying with the body'. It is believed to improve spiritual discipline – by overcoming the sensations of the physical world and focusing on prayer and spiritual growth. It may serve as a way to respect those people around the world who regularly face starvation or malnutrition.

⇨ Self-denial (of food) can help Christians to remember that having what you want is not always the path to happiness.

⇨ Variations of fasting or abstinence are observed by some Roman Catholics on such occasions as Lent or Good Friday; for example, some may strictly avoid meat at this time.

⇨ Most Protestants observe only Easter and Christmas as feast days, and don't follow ritualised fasting.

⇨ Mormons avoid caffeinated and alcoholic beverages.

⇨ The majority of Seventh Day Adventists don't eat meat or dairy products, and are likely to avoid many condiments including mustard. Those that do eat meat don't eat pork.

Judaism

Judaism can be Liberal or Orthodox, based on the degree of adherence to the Jewish laws. 'Kashrut' refers to the laws pertaining to food in the Jewish religion. 'Kosher' means that a food is permitted or 'clean', while anything 'unclean' (such as pork and shellfish) is strictly forbidden. The Jewish 'food laws' originated more than 2,000 years ago and contribute to a formal code of behaviour that reinforces the identity of a Jewish community. Food forms an integral part of religion in life for a practising Jew. Other selected facts include:

⇨ Foods must be prepared in the right way in order to be kosher; for example, animals that provide meat must be slaughtered correctly.

⇨ The consumption of certain foods, including dairy products and fish, is subject to restrictions; for example, there are rules forbidding the mixing and consumption of dairy products with meats.

⇨ Ritualised fasting is also included in Judaism. Yom Kippur – the Day of Atonement – for example, is a Jewish fast that lasts from, approximately, dusk till dusk.

⇨ Jewish feast days include Rosh Hashanah and Passover.

⇨ The Passover commemorates the birth of the Jewish nation. The food eaten helps to tell the story

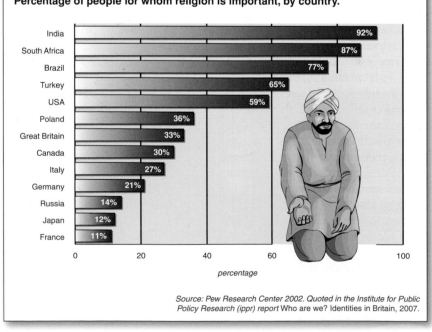

Importance of religion, by country

Percentage of people for whom religion is important, by country.

Country	Percentage
India	92%
South Africa	87%
Brazil	77%
Turkey	65%
USA	59%
Poland	36%
Great Britain	33%
Canada	30%
Italy	27%
Germany	21%
Russia	14%
Japan	12%
France	11%

percentage

Source: Pew Research Center 2002. Quoted in the Institute for Public Policy Research (ippr) report Who are we? Identities in Britain, 2007.

of the Exodus; for example, bitter herbs recall the suffering of the Israelites under Egyptian rule.

Islam

Regulations surrounding food are called 'halal'. Prohibited foods are called 'haram'. It is thought that the Creator turns a deaf ear to a Muslim who eats haram foods. Other selected facts include:

⇨ The list of haram foods includes pork, alcohol, foods that contain emulsifiers (as emulsifiers may be made from animal fats), tinned vegetables that include emulsifiers, frozen vegetables with sauce, particular margarines, and bread or bread products that contain dried yeast.

⇨ Gelatine can be made from pig and, since pork is haram, products containing gelatine are forbidden.

⇨ Caffeinated drinks such as coffee are sometimes considered haram.

⇨ Certain religious dates, such as Eid ul-Fitr, demand fasting from dawn till dusk.

⇨ Some Muslims choose to fast on Mondays or Thursdays or both.

⇨ The month of Ramadan requires mandatory fasting during sunlight hours, as do particular dates of religious significance, such as the ninth day of Zul Hijjah.

Hinduism

People who practise the Hindu religion don't eat meat from animals. They also avoid foods that may have caused pain to animals during manufacture. 'Karma' is believed to be the spiritual load we accumulate or relieve ourselves of during our lifetime. Animals are believed to have spiritual awareness. If a Hindu consumes animal flesh, they accumulate the Karma of that act – which will need to be balanced through good actions and learning in this life or the next. Depending on the level of adherence to this belief, in many cases beef is forbidden, while pork is sometimes restricted or avoided. Selected facts include:

⇨ 'Food is God (Brahman)' is a common Hindu saying. Food is thought to be an actual part of Brahman, rather than simply a Brahman symbol.

⇨ Foods contain energies such as sound waves that can be absorbed by the person who eats them – the Hindu religion takes literally the maxim 'You are what you eat'.

⇨ According to the Hindu religion, violence or pain inflicted on another living thing rebounds on you (Karma).

⇨ In keeping with the aim to avoid violence or pain to any living thing, vegetarianism is advocated, but not compulsory.

Buddhism is more of a life philosophy than a religious doctrine

---

⇨ Prohibited animal products tend to vary from one country or region to the next; for example, duck and crab may be forbidden in one geographical location, but not in another.

⇨ Foodstuffs such as alcohol, onions and garlic are thought to inhibit the Hindu's quest for spiritual enlightenment by exciting the body and leading to acts which may have Karmic impact, and are therefore avoided or restricted.

⇨ While beef is forbidden, dairy products including milk, butter and yoghurt are considered to enhance spiritual purity.

⇨ Fasting depends on the person's caste (or social standing) and the occasion; for example, rules regarding fasting depend on whether the day has religious or personal significance.

Buddhism

The dietary rules of Buddhism, which is more of a life philosophy than a religious doctrine, depend on which branch of Buddhism is practised and in what country. Selected facts include:

⇨ In his lives on Earth, Buddha cycled through various animal forms before he took on the form of a human being – this is why most Buddhists are vegetarian.

⇨ Similarly to the Hindu concept of Karma, Buddhism proposes that violence or pain inflicted on others will rebound on you,

further strengthening the need for a vegetarian lifestyle. Some Buddhists believe that the cause of human aggression is violence against animals.

⇨ Some Buddhists avoid meat and dairy products, while others only shun beef.

⇨ Religious dates vary from one region to the next. Mahayana Buddhism, for example, celebrates three festivals for the birth, enlightenment and death of Buddha, while Theravada Buddhists observe all three events on a single day.

⇨ Buddhist monks tend to fast in the afternoon.

⇨ Buddhist monks and nuns aren't allowed to cultivate, store or cook their own food; instead, they must rely on 'alms', which are donations from believers. This sometimes includes meats, as monks and nuns aren't allowed to ask for specific foods.

⇨ Traditionally, meat from bears, dogs, elephants, horses, hyenas, lions, panthers, snakes and tigers are strictly prohibited to Buddhist monks and nuns.

⇨ This information was provided by the Better Health Channel, a Victorian Government (Australia) website. Material on the Better Health Channel is regularly updated. For the latest version of this information please visit: www.betterhealth.vic.gov.au

© Better Health Channel

Why does religion exist?

Explaining religion and religious beliefs

Problem of explaining religion

Religion is a pervasive and significant cultural phenomenon, so people who study culture and human nature have sought to explain the nature of religion, the nature of religious beliefs, and the reasons why religions exist in the first place. There have been as many theories as theorists, it seems, and while none fully captures what religion is, all offer important insights on the nature of religion and possible reasons why religion has persisted through human history.

Tylor & Frazer – religion is systematised animism & magic

E.B. Tylor and James Frazer are two of the earliest researchers to develop theories of the nature of religion. They defined religion as essentially being the belief in spiritual beings, making it systematised animism. The reason religion exists is to help people make sense of events which would otherwise be incomprehensible by relying on unseen, hidden forces. This inadequately addresses the social aspect of religion, though, depicting religion and animism as purely intellectual moves.

Sigmund Freud – religion is mass neurosis

According to Sigmund Freud, religion is a mass neurosis and exists as a response to deep emotional conflicts and weaknesses. A by-product of psychological distress, Freud argued that it should be possible to eliminate the illusions of religion by alleviating that distress. This approach is laudable for getting us to recognise that there can be hidden psychological motives behind religion and religious beliefs, but his arguments from analogy are weak and too often his position is circular.

People who study culture and human nature have sought to explain the nature of religion, the nature of religious beliefs, and the reasons why religions exist in the first place

---

Emile Durkheim – religion is a means of social organisation

Emile Durkheim is responsible for the development of sociology and wrote that '...religion is a unified system of beliefs and practices relative to sacred things, that is to say, things set apart and forbidden'. His focus was the importance of the concept of the 'sacred' and its relevance to the welfare of the community. Religious beliefs are symbolic expressions of social realities without which religious beliefs have no meaning. Durkheim reveals how religion serves in social functions.

Karl Marx – religion is the opiate of the masses

According to Karl Marx, religion is a social institution which is dependent upon material and economic realities in a given society. With no independent history, it is a creature of productive forces. Marx wrote: 'The religious world is but the reflex of the real world.' Marx argued that religion is an illusion whose chief purpose is to provide reasons and excuses to keep society functioning just as it is. Religion takes our highest ideals and aspirations and alienates us from them.

Mircea Eliade – religion is a focus on the sacred

Key to Mircea Eliade's understanding of religion are two concepts: the sacred and the profane. Eliade says religion is primarily about belief in the supernatural, which for him lies at the heart of the sacred. He does not try to explain away religion and rejects all reductionist efforts. Eliade only focuses on 'timeless forms' of ideas which he says keep recurring in religions all over the world, but in doing so he ignores their specific historical contexts or dismisses them as irrelevant.

Stewart Elliot Guthrie – religion is anthropomorphisation gone awry

Stewart Guthrie argues that religion is 'systematic anthropomorphism' – the attribution of human characteristics to non-human things or events. We interpret ambiguous information as whatever matters most to survival, which means seeing living beings. If we are in the woods and see a dark shape that might be a bear or a rock, it is smart to 'see' a bear. If we are mistaken, we lose little; if we are right, we survive. This conceptual strategy leads to 'seeing' spirits and gods at work around us.

E.E. Evans-Pritchard – religion and emotions

Rejecting most anthropological, psychological, and sociological explanations of religion, E.E. Evans-Pritchard sought a comprehensive explanation of religion that took both its intellectual and social aspects into account. He didn't reach any final answers, but did argue that religion should be regarded as a vital aspect of society, as its 'construct of the heart'. Beyond that, it may not be possible to explain religion in general, just to explain and understand particular religions.

Clifford Geertz – religion as culture and meaning

An anthropologist who describes culture as a system of symbols and actions which convey meaning, Clifford Geertz treats religion as a vital component of cultural meanings. He argues that religion carries symbols which establish especially powerful moods or feelings, help explain human existence by giving it an ultimate meaning, and purport to connect us to a reality that is 'more real' than what we see every day. The religious sphere thus has a special status above and beyond regular life.

Explaining, defining, and understanding religion

Here, then, are some of the principal means of explaining why religion exists: as an explanation for what we don't understand; as a psychological reaction to our lives and surroundings; as an expression of social needs; as a tool of the status quo to keep some people in power and others out; as a focus upon supernatural and 'sacred' aspects of our lives; and as an evolutionary strategy for survival.

Which of these is the 'right' explanation? Maybe we shouldn't try to argue that any one of them is 'right' and instead recognise that religion is a complex human institution. Why assume that religion is any less complex and even contradictory than culture in general? Because religion has such complex origins and motivations, all of the above could serve as a valid response to the question 'Why does religion exist?' None, however, can serve as an exhaustive and complete answer to that question.

We should eschew simplistic explanations of religion, religious beliefs, and religious impulses. They are unlikely to be adequate even in very individual and specific circumstances and they are certainly inadequate when addressing religion generally. Simplistic as these purported explanations may be, though, they all offer helpful insights which can bring us a little closer to understanding what religion is all about.

Does it matter whether we can explain and understand religion, even if only a little bit? Given the importance of religion to people's lives and culture, the answer to this should be obvious. If religion is inexplicable, then significant aspects of human behaviour, belief, and motivation are also inexplicable. We need to at least try to address religion and religious belief in order to get a better handle on who we are as human beings.

A humanist discussion of ethics

Information from the British Humanist Association

A humanist way of thinking about values and ethics

Humanism is an approach to life based on humanity and reason. Humanists recognise that moral values are properly founded on human nature and experience alone: concern for others does not necessarily have an external source, as religions tend to assert. Humanists do not refer to sacred texts or religious authorities when making moral decisions. They do not believe in a life after death that will compensate for earthly suffering by rewarding the good and punishing the bad. Humanists do not believe in a god who gives us moral codes or values, and they base their lives on guiding principles, not dogmatic rules. Despite that, humanists do not believe that basic moral principles are simply matters of personal preference or that they can vary much from place to place or time to time – humanists are not relativists .

Humanists value ideas for which there is evidence, and the things inside and around us that make life worth living. Humanists believe that it is reasonable to enjoy the good things in life if we can do so without harming others or the environment. They think we should all try to live full and happy lives, and that one way to do this is to help other people to do the same. So humanists believe in making responsible choices.

> '…happiness is the only good; …the time to be happy is now, and the way to be happy is to make others so.'
> Robert G Ingersoll, 19th-century American humanist

Humanists value individual freedom, because choice and freedom contribute to human happiness, but they are aware that individual choices, especially lots of individual choices, can have effects on society and cause unintended problems. For example, choosing the sexes of one's children would seem to be a matter of personal choice, not something other people or the Government should interfere in. A small number of such choices, perhaps for medical reasons, would have some good outcomes (fewer children born with inherited illnesses or disabilities) and no bad effects on society. But if everyone chose, and tended to choose one sex above the other (probably, for reasons of tradition, boys), this could have disastrous effects on society and so becomes a matter of moral concern.

Many moral dilemmas today are complicated. Some are new, caused by advances in science or medicine, and changes in the way we live; codes of conduct formulated centuries ago (for example, the Ten Commandments) are not necessarily helpful. Humanists believe that we should review moral codes in the light of our principles and of developments in society and human knowledge. The fact that we can do certain things does not mean that we ought to, but who is to decide what we do? Scientists? Doctors? Politicians? Moral philosophers? Religious leaders? Each individual?

Humanism as a 'set of tools'

Philosophers throughout history have made a distinction between ethics and religion, and have suggested rational arguments for morality. Many philosophers respected by humanists have thought that reason is what distinguishes human beings from animals and that we therefore ought to use reason to solve problems and make life better.

What motivates humanists?

Humanists value happiness, freedom and justice, and will be motivated by the desire to increase these and to leave the world a better place. Humanists believe that we should make the best of the one life we have, and that any rewards and punishments we may receive are here and now. Decent people do generally earn the affection and respect of others, and don't live in fear of disapproval or punishment, and so are generally happier; those who actively care about other people and act on it usually have better relationships and more rewarding lives. Of course the world is full of injustice too – bad people do often prosper and good people suffer. Nevertheless, it isn't naïve or stupid to be good, as some cynics would have it, but actually a sensible and rational response to the

problems of living with other people. Most people do in fact live decent lives and benefit from the fact that others do so too: most of us go about our daily business amongst strangers quite safely, sometimes even meeting with great kindness, compassion and helpfulness.

How should we tackle difficult moral questions?

There are some actions, like murder, that we can generally accept as wrong – we do not have to weigh up the pros and cons every time we are faced with a murder. And, in a democratic nation like the UK , we should obey the law. If humanists think a law is immoral, they work to change it.

Universal social and moral values still leave considerable leeway in their interpretation

---

But there are many moral situations where we do have to think for ourselves. Humanists consider carefully the particular situation and the effects of choices on the happiness or suffering of the people (and sometimes animals) concerned and the wider community. They weigh up the evidence, the probable consequences of the action, and the rights and wishes of those involved, trying to find the kindest course of action or the option that will do the least harm and will not compromise their personal principles or integrity. Often humanist perspectives on moral issues are not very different from those of liberally-minded religious people. However, a humanist view is explicitly based on reason, experience, and empathy and respect for others, rather than on tradition or deference to authority, which often influence religious views.

All this may seem like simple common sense, but it is far from simple in its application. Although many people (including many religious people) do make moral decisions this way, others decide very differently. Some people just obey the teachings of their religion; others accept the conventional wisdom of the day.

Some people adopt rigid rules which they apply in all circumstances; others avoid thinking about moral issues at all or let individual personal preference decide the issue. We are all confronted sometimes with moral choices, perhaps because the situation involves us, or because we are in a position to decide for or advise other people – even voting in an election or shopping might involve making moral choices. As intelligent rational beings, we ought to think about how we make these choices.

Where do moral values come from?

When we are discussing what is right and wrong or making moral decisions, we don't usually worry about where our moral values came from. We are more concerned with what they are and how to apply them in a given situation. If we do stop to consider where they came from, we tend to credit our upbringing or our education. But where did the moral values of our parents and teachers, and of our legislators and rulers, come from?

The most common answer to this is that moral values come from religions, transmitted through sacred texts and priests, and that even the values of non-religious people have been absorbed from the religions around them. Even some non-religious people believe this, and it can be a source of insecurity for them, an area where they are made to feel indebted to a religious culture that they do not share, and where they are patronised or criticised by religious believers. Many people, including some non-believers, worry that a general move away from religious faith will bring about some kind of moral breakdown in society. We have all heard politicians, for example, claiming that more religion in schools will reduce juvenile crime, and we have all read stories about wrongdoers giving up lives of crime because they discovered religion.

But humanists believe that moral values are not dependent on religion and that it is untrue, unfair to non-religious people, and a damaging idea in an increasingly secular society, to assert otherwise. Humanists believe that moral values evolved, and continue to evolve, along with human nature and society, and are indeed based on human nature, experience and society. If human civilisation were to develop all over again, it is highly unlikely that exactly the same religions would develop. But it is very likely that our basic moral principles would be the same, because human beings, who have evolved to live in groups, need the kind of rules which enable us to live together cooperatively and harmoniously. Although anthropologists in the past emphasised the differences between human societies, and xenophobes, racists and religious fundamentalists have always stressed and exploited cultural differences, human beings have in fact much more in common than the superficial differences might suggest. Recent anthropological studies and the work of evolutionary biologists and psychologists have brought home to us how much of our behaviour is universal, including our basic needs and values.

Shared values

Communities can survive and work efficiently, and increase the welfare and happiness of their members, only if the people who live in them co-operate and accept certain principles, based on shared human values. These include: looking after the young and other vulnerable people; valuing the truth and respecting promises; fair allocation of power and property according to some recognised system which includes merit; mutual assistance in defence and disasters; disapproval and punishment of wrongdoers, restraints on violence and killing.

Some of these can be seen in other social animals too, for example mutual help is common in intelligent social animals such as chimpanzees. The human capacity for language has made it possible for us to form-ulate and transmit complex systems of rules, sanctions and rewards. Shared human nature explains the considerable agreement between religions, societies, and ethical and legal systems, about what is good or bad, tolerable or intolerable, moral or immoral, even when they disagree about where their values came from. The Universal Declaration of Human Rights, which has gained wide international acceptance, and which celebrated its fiftieth anniversary in 1998, is underpinned by a belief in shared human needs and values. In England and Wales, a National Forum for Values in Education and the Community formulated a statement of values, which was then given to MORI who polled 3,200 schools, 700 national organisations and 1,500 individuals. About 90% of people agreed with the statement, showing that even within a multicultural and pluralistic society, there is still considerable agreement about moral values. This Statement of Values is now in the revised National Curriculum, and includes statements like: 'We value the environment, both natural and shaped by humanity, as the basis of life and a source of wonder and inspiration', and 'accept our duty to maintain a sustainable environment for future gen-erations', and 'We value relationships as fundamental to the development and fulfil-ment of ourselves and others, and to the good of the community.'

The Golden Rule

Although many of the less important rules vary, all traditions seem to have come up with a version of the 'Golden Rule': 'Do as you would be done by' or 'Treat other people in a way you would like to be treated yourself'. It can be expressed both positively (as above) and negatively ('Do not treat others as you would not like to be treated yourself'). Some people think that the negative versions are more realistic, because it is easier to agree on the things we would not like done to us, and anyone can work out what would cause suffering to another person and then avoid doing it. Humanists have been impressed with the apparently universal nature of this rule and with its egalitarianism and usefulness as a basic principle. It is based on human nature and experience, using our need to be treated well by others and our aspiration to live harmoniously with others as its foundation. It can be worked out by anyone, anywhere, by reference to experience. It does not need to be given to us by a deity.

It is compatible with other well-respected and useful moral principles such as Kant's 'categorical imperative': 'Always treat other people as ends in themselves, never as means to an end' and 'Act only on that maxim which you could will to be universal law.' And John Stuart Mill, in his book *Utilitarianism*, wrote of the Golden Rule: 'To do as you would be done by, and to love your neighbour as yourself, constitute the ideal perfection of utilitarian morality.'

The major world religions share certain values, for example the 'Golden Rule'

Like other very general moral principles, it has been criticised for being empty – it does not give us specific rules of conduct – and for being incomplete – it requires considerable empathy and understanding of others to put it into practice. The playwright George Bernard Shaw joked: 'Don't do to others what you want others to do to you – their tastes may be different.' He had a point, but developing an awareness of the variety of other people's characters and interests is part of growing up and most people are capable of it with a little thought. Humanists do not see the fact that the Golden Rule often needs further reflection before it can be applied as a disadvantage; and its flexibility about actual moral rules and laws would be seen as a positive advantage. It has been called 'a searchlight, not a map', a metaphor which summarises its undogmatic appeal to humanists. The Golden Rule can be the foundation for other principles.

The Golden Rule is also self-correcting. It might seem, if understood superficially, to encourage immoral acts, for example someone who enjoys danger could try to justify putting other people's lives at risk by saying that he would welcome his life being endangered by others. But none of us wants anyone to act towards us without considering our personal wishes and interests, and this aspect of treating others as we would wish to be treated would not permit a danger-lover to take risks with our lives, unless we wanted them to.

Implicitly, the Golden Rule requires kindness and care for the less fortunate, because this is what we would want in their situation, and it discourages lying, bullying and theft, for example, because no one wants to be lied to or bullied or to have their property stolen. It has the virtues of simplicity and clarity and works well in many situations.

Unshared values

Universal social and moral values still leave considerable leeway in their interpretation, and this accounts for disagreements about particular moral questions. Everyone agrees that murder is wrong, but we might disagree about what counts as murder. Abortion? Voluntary euthanasia? Human sacrifice? Killing in war? Killing animals? Everyone agrees that children should be protected and nurtured – but there is considerable disagreement about how exactly this should be done and the best family arrangements in which to achieve it. Religions are the source of much variation. Even within major faiths there are moral disagreements, for example on the merits of pacifism or the use of contraception – deities do not seem to offer moral consistency, despite their reputation for knowing everything.

And there are, of course, some specifically religious values: for example rules about diet, family and marriage, or religious observance. A few religious people define as 'good' anything that a religion or deity or sacred text commands. But most pick and choose from the many conflicting rules in their texts and traditions, and they decide which are the worthwhile rules by using their ability to reason and to learn from experience. Like most other people, including most moral philosophers, they use humanist reasoning and criteria (such as consequences for well-being) when judging right and

wrong. Besides, many religious rules are not about morality at all. (Look at the Ten Commandments – how may of them are actually moral rules?) Many religious rules are based on tradition, or on practices that were useful in the past, but within the religion they have achieved the status of moral values, so that, for example, some groups think it wrong to eat pork or to use contraception. Some religious values are generally, and unthinkingly, accepted as morally worthwhile, for example the Christian edict to 'turn the other cheek', but may, on reflection, be less unambiguously good than appears. Would it be right to turn the other cheek when bullied or exploited? Wouldn't this just encourage bad people to go on behaving badly, to the disadvantage of everyone else?

Morality without religion

Humanist ethics makes human beings solely responsible for working out and implementing moral values and codes. Of course, we do not choose these completely arbitrarily – they must be based on principles that respect the autonomy (or personal freedom) of others and the general welfare. Morality is much more necessary than religion, and in an era of declining religious belief it is a dangerous mistake to confuse the two. Religious faith does motivate and support some people in living better lives, and that is surely a good thing for the community – the more good people there are, the better for all of us. But religion and dogmatic authorities are not essential for morality. Many non-religious people think that it is actually more moral to think for oneself, and to make responsible and independent choices without divine authority or the hope of divine reward in an afterlife. Freely choosing to help someone else could be considered more virtuous than helping someone out of obedience or because you expect a reward.

The words we use

Morality, ethics, values, rights, duties are all words used when people talk about issues of right and wrong, of what we ought and ought not to do. We also talk about fairness and justice (or unfairness and injustice)

and use words like good and bad (or sometimes virtuous and sinful or evil), and legal and illegal. Apart from the last two, which are simply factual statements about what is and is not permitted by law, they are all words which express views about morality or ethics – which mean much the same thing, though we usually use ethics and ethical when being a bit more theoretical.

_____

Are a person's or a society's or a religion's values necessarily good or moral?

These words are sometimes interchangeable, sometimes not. A few examples will illustrate the sometimes subtle differences, and you can think of your own:

⇨ We might say we have a duty to look after our aged parents, or that it is right or good to do so, immoral not to. But it is not illegal to refuse to do so – is it unfair or unjust?
⇨ You might think it is unjust, or unfair, or a bad thing, or immoral that some people have much more money than you, but you do not have a right to their money and it is legal for them to own more than you. Ought it to be?
⇨ Generally, you ought to keep promises, and perhaps you have a right to expect others to keep their promises to you, but it is not normally illegal to break informal promises. Is it immoral or unethical to do so?
⇨ You have the right to life and are entitled to own property and it is illegal to kill you or steal your property. Is this a good thing?
⇨ Are a person's or a society's or a religion's values necessarily good or moral?

Updated July 2006

⇨ The above information is reprinted with kind permission from the British Humanist Association. Visit www.humanism.org.uk for more information.
© _British Humanist Association_

Religion and moral decline

New survey says people think Britain is in moral decline and religion could help

An overwhelming number of people believe that Britain is experiencing a moral decline according to a BBC/ComRes opinion poll for *The Big Questions*, a new BBC belief and ethics programme. 83% of those asked agreed or strongly agreed with that statement, as against only 9% who disagreed.

ComRes telephoned 1000 adults (aged 16+) between 31 August and 2 September 2007. Data were weighted to be representative of all British adults. ComRes is a member of the British Polling Council and abides by its rules.

The majority of people surveyed also believe that religion might have its part to play in putting the situation right. 62% agreed with the statement that religion has an important role to play in the moral guidance of the nation with 29% disagreeing or strongly disagreeing with that statement.

But when asked questions about tackling some of the issues that affect society people gave a mixed response. Asked whether they were prepared to intervene or help a victim a massive majority – 93% – said they would if they saw someone collapsed on the street – although surprisingly, for some, those with no religion were slightly more likely to say they would help – 97% – as opposed to those who said they were Christians – 92%.

Some 61% of people said they would intervene if they saw two children fighting. Although if someone was talking nosily on a mobile phone on a train or bus less than a quarter – 24% – said they would intervene with 76% saying they would not. And if they saw a group of teenagers graffiti-ing a wall only just under a third – 32% – said they would intervene as opposed to more than two-thirds – 68% – who said they would not.

Surprisingly the 16-24 age group was the most likely to agree with the importance of religion in aiding the nation's moral guidance with

68% strongly agreeing or agreeing, which is slightly higher than older generations.

The issues behind the poll will be debated on *The Big Questions* – BBC One's new ethical and religious programme which launches this Sunday 9 September at 10am – with a discussion on whether religion can reverse our moral decline.

The panel for the first *The Big Questions* programme, produced by Mentorn Oxford, makers of BBC One's *Question Time*, is: journalist Amanda Platell; Jonathan Bartley, co-director of the theological think-thank Ekklesia; Dr Jeevan Deol, an academic specialising in religion and politics; and the scientist and broadcaster Dr Alice Roberts.

In an initial comment on the survey, Ekklesia co-director Simon Barrow said: 'Overall this seems like good news. The great majority of people of all outlooks are seeking for a better society and recognising that consumption and technology aren't enough. The results look like ethical commitment rather than simple "moral panic". But there remains a gap between intentions and behaviour, and the lack of moral consensus in an increasingly diverse society poses a challenge.'

On the role of religion, Barrow added: 'On the one hand it is clear that people of faith do not have a monopoly on morality, and almost a third of the population reject religious influence. On the other hand, a majority believe religion can have a positive effect – but the real question is "what kind of religion?" and indeed "what do we mean by religion?"'

The Ekklesia co-director said there were no grounds for triumphalism in the survey, either by advocates or detractors of religion.

He added that whereas the survey's approach might suggest that 'morality' is primarily about personal virtue and decision making, 'it is also about the structural questions of

wealth, ecology, violence and human dignity. And effective ethics means acting as persons-in-relation, not "heroic individuals".'

Concluded Barrow: 'What we need is not a vague debate about values, but people from different backgrounds and outlooks who are prepared to work together to build concrete alternative practices like hospitality, civility, non-violence, economic sharing, reconciliation and so on. It is about making a different world possible, not just talking about it.'

Could the moral guidance provided by religion help to combat social ills such as binge drinking?

Ekklesia believes that the Christian churches can play a positive role in encouraging ethical collaboration, but that if they are true to their Gospel message they should not be seeking sectional advantage or moral superiority.

'What makes morality is working together, not against each other or in disregard of the needs of the other. Recognising common humanity is part of the search for a justice and peace that Christians call "communion",' Barrow said.
7 September 2007

⇨ Information from Ekklesia. Visit www.ekklesia.co.uk for more information.

© *Ekklesia*

Crisis of faith?

Religions united in struggling with falling attendances

What explains the decline in traditional religious observance in Britain, and is it being replaced by alternative or 'secular' religions? New research shows that the decline in observance extends across all religions, including Islam, and that we do not necessarily become more religious as we get older. It also throws up a challenge to all organised religions, as Robert Pigott explains.

By Robert Pigott

'The Church' to many English parishioners – and we're all in a parish whether we realise it or not – is embodied by the solid stone structure in the centre of the community. Unchanging and historic (some go back a thousand years, the sites longer still) the buildings have served to conceal the changes affecting religion in Britain. Great tidal flows in belief, a sense of 'belonging' to the Church, and attendance at its services, have washed through Britain's parish churches leaving them apparently unaffected, stolidly working through the Christian year in liturgy often dating back 350 years.

But the tidal currents shifting religion in Britain seem more profound now than at any time since the Reformation. The latest shift is not new: the steep decline in church attendance in England has been going on at least since the 1950s, and the desertion of Welsh chapels started earlier still. However, for institutions characterised by stable beliefs and practices, and histories measured in centuries, what is happening now is virtually a revolution.

Sociologists such as Dr David Voas of the Cathie Marsh Centre for Census and Survey Research at Manchester University and Dr Alasdair Crockett of the Institute for Social and Economic Research at the University of Essex have studied both trends in an attempt to create a general theory to explain religious change. Their ESRC-funded research project identified three components of religion among people – their underlying belief, their sense of affiliation to a particular faith or denomination, and their propensity to attend services. They have isolated a number of factors working on these elements of faith. In summary they are: how far parents pass on their faith to their children; the experiences and pressures on particular generations (the baby boomers perhaps); and what the simple effects of getting older can do to one's sense of the eternal.

Sociological studies trying to tease out cause and effect in religion have tended to be snapshots of people's beliefs and practices at a given historical moment. Rarely (with the exception of Gill in 1999) have they followed groups of individuals to obtain a more dynamic picture. Voas and Crockett used the British Household Panel Survey (BHPS, 1991 onwards) in order to achieve this 'longitudinal' view. They paid particular attention to the large group whose responses were contained in both the first and the last 'waves' of research, as the clearest illustration of change among individuals over time. They also singled out the responses of children whose parents' data were included, and those of couples. The results were intriguing.

Firstly, how far are parents responsible for passing on their own faith to their children, and how significant is it if they have different beliefs and practices? Here Voas and Crockett's findings are startlingly straightforward. If both parents attend services or at least identify with a religion, then there's a virtually 50/50 likelihood of their children doing so too. If only one of the parents attends, the likelihood is halved to 25 per cent, and if neither of the parents attends or 'belongs', the chances of the children doing so are negligible.

> **If both parents attend services or at least identify with a religion, then there's a virtually 50/50 likelihood of their children doing so too**

The findings may be significant for those faiths where religion and identity are closely intertwined. Perhaps the central issue of debate and controversy in the Jewish community is between traditionalists who insist that the community's continued health relies on its religious devotion, and more liberal-minded secularists who believe it is possible to be 'fully Jewish' by preserving Jewish culture. If the traditionalists are right, a slippage in attendance at synagogue, or the observance of religious festivals, could have a far-reaching effect.

One of the religious changes most people will have noticed in recent decades is the increasing presence of Islam in Britain, and of its minarets on city skylines. Voas and Crockett found, however, that although ethnic minorities – including Islam – play an increasingly important part in British religious life, downward trends in belief and attendance are similar to the rest of the population. Mosques are often controlled by 'first generation' immigrants to the UK. They are frequently served by imams trained in traditionalist madrassahs in Pakistan who speak only rudimentary English and hold services in minority languages, such as Urdu or Bangladeshi. Indeed they have faced some criticism, including from within Islam, for their failure to address a younger generation, who speak English and demonstrate a wish to link their faith with life in a modern Western setting.

Voas and Crockett's research makes clear that how children are brought up will heavily influence whether they will later identify with a religion. It also shows that once they are adults, they will be pretty resistant to change. But what about the simple effects of growing older? Are parish churches populated by predominantly older people because we become more religious the nearer we get to the end of life?

Data from the BHPS suggest that parish churches are populated mostly by older people not so much because we become more religious the nearer we get to the end of life, but because they belong to a generation of people more religious than ones born more recently.

Such 'cohort' effects may explain the dramatic decline in Welsh chapel-going. The biggest denomination, the Presbyterian Church of Wales, had 600 ministers and almost 1,500 chapels in 1950; but by 2004 all but 775 chapels had been demolished or turned into houses or pubs, and there were just 93 ministers attending to a diminished flock.

One explanation is that while Welsh-speaking parents continued to attend, a generation that left for the Second World War and brought back English and a new sense of social mobility deserted the pews.

The traditional theory by which sociologists have explained growing secularisation suggests that growing prosperity – with better education and health – erodes the need for the support religious faith offers. It is not that people lose their faith, so much as stop going to church, with predictable effects on their children.

Out of this idea has grown the thesis of 'believing without belonging', advanced particularly by Professor Grace Davie of Exeter University. It suggests that people's religious beliefs are more robust than their sense of affiliation, or their attendance at services. However, Voas and Crockett found evidence in the BHPS that religious belief was declining at least as quickly as churchgoing. They also argue that fewer people now have real faith than passively 'belong' to a religion.

Perhaps that is what's behind the big surge in churchgoing in parts of Britain at Christmas, among people who show little interest during the rest of the year. In another study, David Voas found that dioceses with large suburban populations had the biggest proportional increase among people who did not go to church normally but evidently saw a service as part of 'the Christmas package'. There was an interesting north-south split, with 'Christmas tourists' boosting attendance in Guildford diocese by 200 per cent, but Manchester seeing only a 20 per cent increase.

So if orthodox religious belief is declining, what, if anything, is replacing it?

There are signs of a greater readiness to acknowledge a more generalised 'spirituality', that is separate from religious beliefs. *The Spiritual Revolution* by Paul Heelas and Linda Woodhead of Lancaster University, found that alternative 'holistic' practices such as yoga, meditation and reiki accounted for around two or three per cent of the population in Kendal in Cumbria, a similar proportion to Voas and Crockett's study. But holistic spiritual practices had grown by 300 per cent in Kendal during the 1990s. The town was chosen for its close fit with average religious practices in Britain, including the decline in churchgoing from 11 to 7.9 per cent of the population over the same period. Heelas and Woodhead concluded that if the change continued at the same rate, 'spirituality' would grow from its current toe-hold to eclipse Christianity within the next 30 years.

The decline in religious belief and practice in Britain is matched in other developed countries. It seems significant that of the 20 countries that score most highly in the UN's Human Development Index, 19 are very secular. The exception is the United States, where a 2002 Pew Global Attitudes Project found 60 per cent of people acknowledging that religion had a very important role in their lives and more than half describing their view of atheists as 'unfavourable'.

The American exception to the assumption that secularisation follows prosperity has produced an alternative 'free-market' or 'supply-side' theory. It holds that the competition between many religious denominations in America makes churches more responsive to people's spiritual needs, and leaves few excluded from the market.

Alasdair Crockett and David Voas now intend to use longitudinal data similar to that provided by the BHPS to study religious change in seven industrial nations including the United States. By testing the same factors affecting religious behaviour – parent-child transmission, the effects of ageing, etc. – in countries where the outcome has been different, they hope to examine more closely how each of them works. So, for example, is the likelihood of parents passing on their faith to children explained by what goes on inside families or the environment they live in? Enriching our understanding of these variables should help to develop a general theory to explain religious change.

The Church of England is among those in apparently secularising societies looking for ways of enhancing their public appeal by adapting the way they do business. The approach has necessarily been fairly experimental, even piecemeal. Anglican leaders will await a refined theory of religious change with as much interest as any.

July 2006

Empty pews are an increasingly common sight in churches

⇨ Taken from the July 2006 edition of the ESRC's monthly publication *The Edge* and reprinted with permission. For more information on this and other issues, visit their website at www.esrc.ac.uk

© Economic and Social Research Council

One in seven adults attends church every month

Potential congregation of 3 million just waiting to be asked

One in seven adults in the UK attends a Christian church each month, with nearly 3 million more people saying they would attend church if only they were asked, one of the largest surveys of churchgoing in the UK reveals today (3 April 2007).

The findings of the in-depth survey by Christian relief and development agency Tearfund also show that, contrary to the UK's secular image, Christianity is still the dominant faith in the UK. Over half (53%) or 26.2 million adults claim to be Christian.

Churchgoing in the UK – one of the few surveys to track monthly church attendance and the likelihood of non-churchgoers attending – shows that 7.6 million adults go to church each month and one in 10 adults attends weekly. One in four (12.6 million) attend at least once a year.

Unexpectedly, the survey shows that 3 million people who have stopped going to church or who have never been in their lives, would consider attending given the right invitation.

Dr Elaine Storkey, President of Tearfund, who also lectures in Theology at the University of Oxford, says, 'This survey is a valuable contribution to exploring what people in Britain today think about church, why people attend and crucially, what is most likely to encourage people to make a connection with church.'

7.6 million adults go to church each month and one in 10 adults attends weekly

---

Matthew Frost, Chief Executive of Tearfund, says, 'What is clear from this survey is that the UK is holding firmly to the Christian faith. This is a great encouragement to Tearfund – we tackle poverty and injustice in partnership with churches in some of the world's poorest communities and we could not do it without the volunteers, prayer and money from churches throughout the UK supporting other churches around the world in the fight against poverty.'

Churchgoing in the UK also reveals that:
⇨ 22% of Londoners attend church each month.
⇨ 1 million adults attend ethnic minority Christian churches.

⇨ 48% of adults of black ethnic origin attend church monthly.
⇨ Other faiths account for 6% of religious attendance.
⇨ 66% of the population still have no connection with church.

Writing in a foreword to the report, Rev Dr Stephen Croft, the Archbishops' Missioner and leader of Fresh Expressions, says, 'There is significant encouragement for churches in this Tearfund research. A very substantial part of the population in the UK still attend church regularly or occasionally during the year. Christians are not (as yet) the tiny minority that some would suggest. This statistic alone has major implications not only for the churches but for public debate and public policy.'

Dr Croft says the report highlights a clear opportunity for churches to attract new members by tapping into the nearly 3 million (6% of UK adults) who are likely to go to church in future. The survey revealed that a personal invite, family or a friend attending or difficult personal circumstances, are most likely to encourage people into church.

Tearfund's research offers a different perspective than the English Church Census, with more than 7,000 people throughout the UK interviewed in detail, both those who do not attend church as well as those who do, compared to the Census' snapshot of church attendance in England on a given Sunday. Tearfund's research finds that 9% of adults in England attend church at least once a week compared to 6% in church on a typical Sunday in the Census.

Churchgoing in the UK also shows that Christianity today has a multi-cultural face with nearly 1 million adults attending ethnic majority churches. Regular churchgoing is particularly high among adults

of black ethnic origin at 48% – over three times the proportion among white adults (15%). The largest denominations among ethnic majority churches overall are Pentecostal (23%), Roman Catholic (23%) and Church of England/ Anglican (19%).

66% of the population still have no connection with church

The survey highlights that the biggest challenge remains people opting out of religion altogether. Two-thirds of UK adults (66%) or 32.2 million people have no connection with church at present (or with any other religion).

Surprisingly, Greater London has one of the highest numbers of regular churchgoers (22%), second only to Northern Ireland (45%), despite being a multi-cultural city with more people of 'other faiths' (20%) than anywhere else in the country.

The devoted core of regular churchgoers are women (19% attend at least monthly); over 55 years old (22%); from social class AB (21%) and those of black ethnic origin (48%).

Rev Lynda Barley, Head of Research and Statistics for the Church of England Archbishop's Council, comments, 'Britain at the beginning of the twenty-first century is a nation seeking identity. At first glance the past has been left behind to wholeheartedly embrace individual choice and secular consumerism prominently among its modern-day

gods. But research is beginning to show that there is more, far more, going on out of apparent sight in everyday life in Britain today.'

Note

Churchgoing in the UK represents the main findings from research conducted by TNS on behalf of Tearfund among a representative poll of 7,000 adults in the UK, aged 16 or over, between 8 February and 5 March 2006. A sample of this magnitude provides robust evidence on churchgoing behaviour. For more information see www.tearfund.org
3 April 2007

⇨ The above information is reprinted with kind permission from Tearfund. Visit www.tearfund.org for more information.

© *Tearfund*

Church of England still valid as state religion?

Information from Reuters

By Paul Majendie

The row over gay adoption has thrown into sharp focus the Church of England's unique role as the country's state religion as Britain grapples with the pressures of a multi-cultural society.

'Church and state should be separated'

The Church is already battling internal divisions over gay priests and women bishops, struggling to impose any authority in an increasingly secular society and facing a steady drop in congregations.

Even Prince Charles, who one day will be Supreme Governor of the Church of England, wonders whether he should be Defender of Faith rather than Defender of The Faith to mirror the racial and religious make-up of 21st-century Britain.

The Church of England became the established church of the land

after the 16th century Reformation when Henry VIII broke ties with the Pope in Rome so he could divorce his first wife.

Now, in a high stakes clash between church and state, Archbishop of Canterbury Rowan Williams has sprung to the defence of the Roman Catholic Church.

The Catholics want to be excused from new anti-discrimination laws which they say could force their adoption agencies to place children with gay couples.

Williams, spiritual head of the world's 77 million Anglicans, argued: 'The rights of conscience cannot be made subject to legislation, however well-meaning.'

So who then does he owe allegiance to?

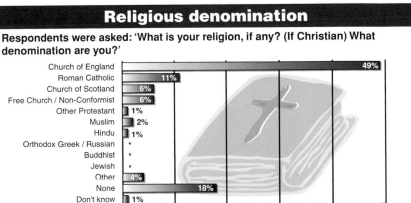

Religious denomination

Respondents were asked: 'What is your religion, if any? (If Christian) What denomination are you?'

	%
Church of England	49%
Roman Catholic	11%
Church of Scotland	6%
Free Church / Non-Conformist	6%
Other Protestant	1%
Muslim	2%
Hindu	1%
Orthodox Greek / Russian	*
Buddhist	*
Jewish	*
Other	4%
None	18%
Don't know	1%

% 0   10   20   30   40   50

Asterisk indicates finding of less than 0.5%, but more than 0. Source: Ipsos MORI. Poll conducted 17-22 May 2001.

Williams said: 'What's at stake ultimately is whether the church is answerable finally to the state as the only court of appeal or whether the church can rightly appeal to other sources for its moral compass.'

Allegiance to the Crown

Long gone are the days when Britain had an empire and its missionaries helped colonise vast areas of the world.

But Anglican vicars still swear allegiance to the Crown. They are paid by the state for working in prisons, hospitals and the armed forces.

To left-wing firebrand Tony Benn, the set-up is an outrageous anachronism.

The deep-seated English affection for tradition and continuity could well kick in to save the Church

---

'Church and state should be separated,' the veteran socialist told Reuters. 'The Church is our oldest nationalised industry. No government should be controlled by religion. It is totally undemocratic, it is all rubbish.'

What then is the alternative in Britain where the threat from radical Islam has provoked soul-searching over how much ethnic communities should be assimilated into mainstream society?

Mainstream Muslims are reluctant to call for the disestablishment of the Church.

'While it is not our faith, the Church of England serves a useful purpose in reminding people about the importance of religion in public life,' a spokesman for the Muslim Council of Britain told Reuters.

The deep-seated English affection for tradition and continuity could well kick in to save the Church.

Reflecting on the way people turn to the Church for officially sanctioned solace in time of trauma, religious commentator Clifford Longley said: 'It has this fire brigade function when things go haywire and tragedy strikes.

'But the problem of keeping the church going is what do you do when they aren't any fires, any cathartic moments?

'Once you remove an established church, what moves into the vacuum? In America it was worship of the flag. The flag is treated by Americans as holy and not to be profaned.'
25 January 2007

⇨ The above information is reprinted with kind permission from Reuters. Visit www.reuters.com for more information.

© Reuters

Only one in six children is now baptised

By Steve Doughty, Social Affairs Correspondent

The Church of England has launched a campaign to make baptisms more popular after it was revealed that the number has halved in 15 years.

Fewer than one in six of all infants is now baptised and in major cities the number has fallen to one in ten.

A book of guidance is being sent to clergy asking them to modernise their approach. One suggestion is that they make cohabiting couples feel more welcome, with a view to encouraging them to become regular churchgoers.

The guide says: 'For some families today, the baptism of a child represents an opportunity for the first public acknowledgement of the parents' relationship. Churches can use this as an opportunity to promote marriage.'

Just over 15 per cent of babies were christened into the C of E in 2005. The total of 93,000 Anglican baptisms was just over half the 184,000 as recently as 1990, they revealed.

In the early 1930s seven out of ten of all children were baptised into the C of E. More than a third were still christened in the early 1980s. Latest figures show that the popularity of christenings remains high in the countryside and some provincial towns but that in London and Birmingham fewer than one in ten babies are baptised.

The guidance, *Connecting with Baptism*, showed that the highest number of christenings is in Carlisle, where more than 40 per cent of babies are baptised.

'Significantly more infant baptisms as a proportion of births take place in rural dioceses such as Carlisle, Hereford and Lincoln,' it said.

The drop in baptisms mirrors a long-term decline in church attendance overall. The C of E saw its figures for Sunday attendance drop below the million mark at around the turn of the millennium. Roman Catholic churches in much of the country have also seen a fall.

However large-scale immigration from Eastern Europe has meant some Catholic churches in London are overflowing on a Sunday.

⇨ This article first appeared in the *Daily Mail*, 3 October 2007.

© 2007 Associated Newspapers Ltd

Religion: who needs it?

Information from the *New Statesman*

By Bryan Appleyard

We live in times where the power of religious belief can often appear terrifying. Yet in many countries religion is declining as dramatically as it is thriving in others. In this special issue we ask how important religion still is in the modern world – and can it survive in a future where science and technology are the gods? Bryan Appleyard begins in Britain – and finds the church in trouble.

British jurors are offered an alternative when they are sworn in. Either they can swear on the Bible or any other holy book or they can 'affirm'. The latter option is plainly for atheists or the secular-minded. During a recent spell of jury service at the Old Bailey, I saw one woman affirm. All of the rest – a sample, in my presence, of perhaps 40 people – swore on the Bible.

And yet we are, seemingly, a secular nation. Church attendance is at a historic low – just over four million – and falling at a steady 2 per cent a year. On this basis, the figure will be roughly 2.5 million by 2020. By then, fewer than 250,000 will be under 20, implying an even more vertiginous drop thereafter as dying churchgoers are not replaced.

There are important nuances and exceptions hidden behind these figures to which I shall return. But the broad picture is irrefutable: the church in Britain is on its deathbed.

So why did we all pick up the New Testament and swear in the name of God rather than affirm in the name of ourselves? The obvious answer is that we saw ourselves as 'cultural Christians'. Most people in Britain do. In sharp contrast to church attendance figures, something like four out of every five people say they feel an affiliation with an established church and 72 per cent say they are Christian. This probably just means that, seeking some way to mark births, marriages, deaths and the proceedings of justice, we turn to the most generally accepted form of external authority.

It certainly seems to amount to little more than that, for not only do the British not go to church, they also don't seem to have a clue what Christianity is. A *Reader's Digest* poll last year found that only 48 per cent of us know that Easter marks the death and resurrection of Christ. In such a context, even describing ourselves as 'cultural Christians' is going too far. Perhaps we should simply say that, once in a while, being mildly stricken by a need to assent to some form of belonging which, at least in theory, transcends our atomised, consumerised lives, we turn to the fusty institutions of what somebody once said was our national faith and, having done so, at once turn away in embarrassment.

> **In sharp contrast to church attendance figures, something like four out of every five people say they feel an affiliation with an established church**

Enough said? Well, no. First, let me deal with the nuances and exceptions to those figures. The black churches are booming. Although black people represent only 2 per cent of the population, they account for two-thirds of the churchgoers in London, and 7 per cent across the country. In Plaistow, in the East End, Glory House, founded by Nigerian immigrants in 1993, attracts congregations of 2,000 or more. Black church membership as a whole has grown by almost a fifth in recent years. In the Birmingham area, there are around 150 black-majority churches serving some 30,000 followers.

Indeed, immigrant and minority communities tend to display much greater religious devotion. Poles and Portuguese pack their local Catholic churches and crowds flood

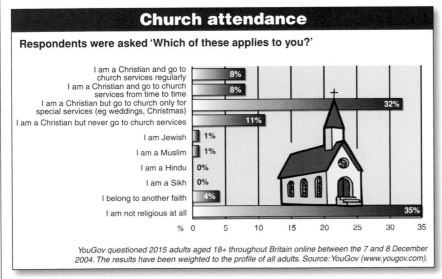

Church attendance

Respondents were asked 'Which of these applies to you?'

	%
I am a Christian and go to church services regularly	8%
I am a Christian and go to church services from time to time	8%
I am a Christian but go to church only for special services (eg weddings, Christmas)	32%
I am a Christian but never go to church services	11%
I am Jewish	1%
I am a Muslim	1%
I am a Hindu	0%
I am a Sikh	0%
I belong to another faith	4%
I am not religious at all	35%

% 0   5   10   15   20   25   30   35

YouGov questioned 2015 adults aged 18+ throughout Britain online between the 7 and 8 December 2004. The results have been weighted to the profile of all adults. Source: YouGov (www.yougov.com).

out of the Ukrainian Cathedral in London, mingling with the shoppers at nearby Selfridges. It is white British Christianity that is specifically in decline; in other racial and national groups the faith is thriving. This disparity can be globalised; religion is thriving in third world countries and declining in most of the first world.

In response to the British problem, there have been various initiatives to revitalise our native faith. There is Faithworks, led by Steve Chalke; this organisation first lured Tony Blair into coming fairly clean about his faith during the last election campaign. He has since come even cleaner by saying he will be judged by God for his conduct of the Iraq war. Most famously – and controversially – there has been the Alpha course. This originated and is still based at Holy Trinity, a C of E church immediately behind the Catholic Brompton Oratory in London. There it attracts the wealthy young consumers of Knightsbridge, though now it is a global enterprise. Alpha people are well trained in the black art of public relations and the course has, as a result, become a media standby for all discussions about the decline of religion and the enduring conflict between God and Mammon.

But what is most interesting about Alpha is not, in the context of British observance, its religious orthodoxy, but its transatlantic, neocharismatic style. Alpha originated in a practice known as the Toronto Blessing, a frequently violent and always emotional conversion or initiation procedure which, to Anglican eyes, looks more like American hot gospelry than quiet British observance. It appeals to the senses and to immediate experience rather than to prayer and meditation. For all Alpha's success – two million Britons have completed its courses – this measure alone can do nothing to stem the decline in UK church attendance. But it does demonstrate the gulf between what might work in an affluent, distracted, ill-educated society and what is being offered by the mainstream churches.

This in turn points to the real issue of the British and, for that matter, western European decline

in formal religious observance. Is it an inevitable accompaniment to increasing affluence? This is the most important nuance to the figures because it calls into question the exact meaning of the gaps between a 'cultural' faith that might just make us pick up a New Testament in court, full-blooded faith, and thoroughgoing atheism. Is cultural faith merely a transit camp on the way to secularism or is it a temporary lapse from which we can be saved by a suitably energetic evangelical movement or, indeed, by a sufficiently dire external threat? In this last context, how many of us can be sure we would not utter a prayer if we knew a nuclear strike was incoming?

Atheist parents are sending their children to Sunday school, and there is a generalised anxiety about our ability to pass anything on to our children if all we share is a condition of absolute disbelief

---

America is the big problem for both sides in this debate. Secularists, who argue that affluence as well as scientific and technological progress will inevitably banish religion from the world, have to deal with the awkward fact that the US, the richest and most technically advanced nation on earth, is also among the most religious – though secularists may reasonably respond that religion does not seem to make the US an especially moral nation.

America is crucial, especially for Britain, which is always seen as a mid-Atlantic nation, halfway between Catholic Europe and Protestant America. In this context, it is important to understand that both the secular and religious views of what is going on there seem to

require the same thing: a rationale for social cohesion. Religion in the US has long been seen as the *sine qua non* of the stable society. Equally, the postwar European settlement has been based on an ideal of secular, cultural integration as the only way of escaping from the nightmares of the past. There is, it is thought, a common European culture that transcends the blood-soaked religious and nationalistic divisions of the past.

The British seem to want neither American religiosity nor further integration with Europe. What, then, do we want?

Maybe full-blown secularism, but the evidence is against this. The first exhibit is history. There has never been a fully secular society and, after the failure of communism's attempt to extirpate religion from Russia and China, it is hard to imagine there ever will be. Japan is often quoted as the most secular country in the world, but only by people who don't understand the tight links between its national identity and its religion. You don't need faith in Japan to be religious; you just need to want to belong, and many Japanese do so through some degree of observance of Buddhist and Shinto rites. The evidence in Europe is more complex but far from clear. Secularity undoubtedly has a firmer grip here than anywhere else, but Christianity, even if only in its cultural manifestation, is still a potent presence. Large parts of eastern Europe, of course, remain firmly and explicitly Christian.

The second exhibit is the actual behaviour of the British. The baby-boomer middle classes are displaying unease with their children's religious

Statistics show that more Britons believe in ghosts than own a Bible

ignorance. Atheist parents are sending their children to Sunday school, and there is a generalised anxiety about our ability to pass anything on to our children if all we share is a condition of absolute disbelief. If T. S. Eliot was right and our culture is an expression of our religion, without religion we must be without culture. This may seem absurd to the secular-minded, but they have yet to come up with a response in the form of a persuasive notion of a post- or non-religious culture.

---

72 per cent of Britain's population consider themselves Christian. However, 48 per cent do not understand that Easter marks the death and resurrection of Jesus

---

The real behavioural evidence, however, is nothing to do with the half-hearted pursuit of orthodoxy. It is the increasingly desperate pursuit of any kind of transcendence. The Alpha course is an aspect of this. It presents Christianity as therapeutic and self-actualising in an attempt to appeal to precisely those values that most preoccupy the modern imagination. Yet it does so in the face of enormous competition. Alternative medicine, New Age beliefs, counselling, psychotherapy, self-help books, popularised philosophy and countless other phenomena all attest to the contemporary desire to do something other than get, spend and, occasionally, vote. Anomie, the condition of normlessness and alienation first defined by Émile Durkheim, is real, as is the corresponding desire to escape its clutches. In the self-centred society, the escape into useful community action does not work. Instead, we escape into a variety of ersatz spiritualities.

To say that none of this constitutes a religion in any organised or coherent sense is to miss the point. Religion, in my view, can only be properly understood as something

like emotion: an innate condition of our existence and a form of our perception of the world. When its expression is denied or refused in one direction, it will simply find another. An inability to grasp this explains the deep and abiding failure of the secular imagination to grasp the dynamics of the post-cold war world in which religion has come to play such a huge part.

I would guess that at the Old Bailey we mostly swore by God because, in the face of all that sombre ceremony, we quietly accepted the demand – however unreasonable – that we belong to something larger than ourselves. I'd like to say it was a fleeting thing, scarcely worth mentioning: a mere habit, a reflex, perhaps even an embarrassment. I'd like to, but I'm afraid I can't.
Bryan Appleyard writes for the Sunday Times. www.bryanappleyard.com

Faith by numbers
⇨ Fewer than two million people regularly attend Church of England services; the number who say they are C of E has dropped 40 per cent since 1983.
⇨ 72 per cent of Britain's population

consider themselves Christian. However, 48 per cent do not understand that Easter marks the death and resurrection of Jesus.
⇨ The largest non-Christian religious group is Muslims: 1.6 million in Britain.
⇨ 34 per cent of British Muslims are under the age of 16.
⇨ 36 per cent of Britons aged 18-34 define themselves as atheist or agnostic.
⇨ Among the over-65s only 11 per cent say they are non-religious
⇨ The population of the north-east of England includes the largest percentage of Christians (80 per cent); London's has the lowest (58 per cent).
⇨ Twice as many British women as men aged 20-29 are regular churchgoers.
⇨ More Britons believe in ghosts than own a Bible.
Research by Kathy Haywood
10 April 2006

⇨ The above information is reprinted with kind permission from the *New Statesman*. Visit www.newstatesman.com for more information.
© *New Statesman*

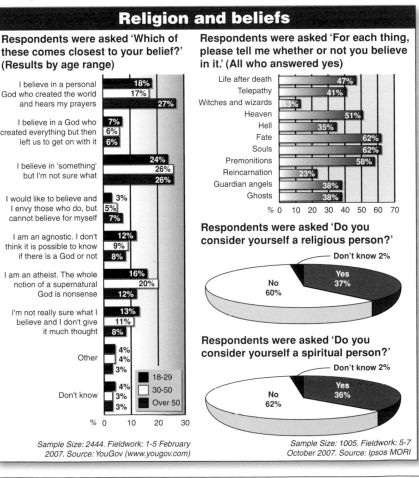

Religion and beliefs

Respondents were asked 'Which of these comes closest to your belief?' (Results by age range)

I believe in a personal God who created the world and hears my prayers — 18% / 17% / 27%

I believe in a God who created everything but then left us to get on with it — 7% / 6% / 6%

I believe in 'something' but I'm not sure what — 24% / 26% / 26%

I would like to believe and I envy those who do, but cannot believe for myself — 3% / 5% / 7%

I am an agnostic. I don't think it is possible to know if there is a God or not — 12% / 9% / 8%

I am an atheist. The whole notion of a supernatural God is nonsense — 16% / 20% / 12%

I'm not really sure what I believe and I don't give it much thought — 13% / 11% / 8%

Other — 4% / 4% / 3%

Don't know — 4% / 3% / 3%

% 0 10 20 30

Legend: 18-29 / 30-50 / Over 50

Sample Size: 2444. Fieldwork: 1-5 February 2007. Source: YouGov (www.yougov.com)

Respondents were asked 'For each thing, please tell me whether or not you believe in it.' (All who answered yes)

Life after death — 47%
Telepathy — 41%
Witches and wizards — 13%
Heaven — 51%
Hell — 35%
Fate — 62%
Souls — 62%
Premonitions — 58%
Reincarnation — 23%
Guardian angels — 38%
Ghosts — 38%

% 0 10 20 30 40 50 60 70

Respondents were asked 'Do you consider yourself a religious person?'
Don't know 2%
Yes 37%
No 60%

Respondents were asked 'Do you consider yourself a spiritual person?'
Don't know 2%
Yes 36%
No 62%

Sample Size: 1005. Fieldwork: 5-7 October 2007. Source: Ipsos MORI

Majority views religion as force for good

By Jonathan Petre, Religion Correspondent

Most people believe that religion is a force for good and should play an important part in national life, according to research published today at the launch of a counter-attack against secularism.

The survey by Theos, a newly-formed religious think tank backed by the leaders of the Anglican and Roman Catholic Churches, also found young people were less hostile to faith than their elders.

Launching its initiative, which will refuel an already inflammatory debate over the role of Christianity and the State, Theos attacked 'public atheism' and called for a 'fight-back' for faith.

The Archbishop of Canterbury, Dr Rowan Williams, and Cardinal Cormac Murphy-O'Connor, the head of Catholics in England and Wales, said that religion had rarely been so significant or so misunderstood.

They argued that those who campaigned for the removal of religion from national life were themselves guilty of an 'intolerant faith position'.

In a joint foreword to a Theos report entitled *Doing God: a Future for Faith in the Public Square*, they said that religiously-inspired activity in the public arena could be 'radically inclusive'.

The report argued against confining faith to the private sphere and predicted that religion would play an increasingly crucial role because of growing interest in its part in promoting happiness and well-being as well as its impact on civil society and the politics of identity.

The Archbishop and the Cardinal referred in their foreword to Leo Tolstoy, who resisted the conventional wisdom of his day that religion could not be taken seriously by educated people because of his growing perplexity about the meaning and value of life.

They said that people today were experiencing similar perplexity and asked: 'As a society, we must decide how we will respond to this moment of collective confusion – can we go on living as before? Or, like Tolstoy, will we reassess the importance of faith to individuals and society?'

The Church leaders' remarks follow rows over faith schools, the wearing of crosses and the publication of an attack on religion by Richard Dawkins, the Oxford University professor and 'militant' atheist, in his book *The God Delusion*.

But a poll of 1,008 adults for Theos by CommunicateResearch found that 53 per cent of Britons agreed that, on balance, religion is a force for good, compared with 39 per cent who disagreed. An even higher proportion, 58 per cent, agreed that Christianity had an important role to play in public life, while 37 per cent did not.

The survey also found that young adults were least likely to agree with Prof Dawkins's assessment that religion is one of the world's great evils, comparable to the smallpox virus but harder to eradicate.

Of 18- to 24-year-olds, just over a third, 36 per cent, agreed with this statement, in contrast to 44 per cent of 35- to 44-year-olds and 47 per cent of 55- to 64-year-olds.

Paul Woolley, the director of Theos, said: 'It is clear that society is embarking on rapid desecularisation. It is no longer considered bold, brave and brilliant to argue that religion is an infantile delusion.'

But Terry Sanderson, of the National Secular Society, said the report was 'a recipe for disaster'.

'The British public does not want its life to be dictated by religious institutions, which it sees as nasty, small-minded and controlling.'

8 November 2006

© Telegraph Group Limited, London 2006

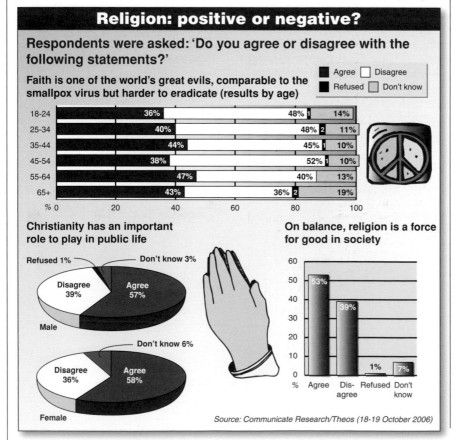

Religion: positive or negative?

Respondents were asked: 'Do you agree or disagree with the following statements?'

Faith is one of the world's great evils, comparable to the smallpox virus but harder to eradicate (results by age)

Legend: Agree, Disagree, Refused, Don't know

Age	Agree	Disagree	Don't know
18-24	36%	48% 1	14%
25-34	40%	48% 2	11%
35-44	44%	45%	10%
45-54	38%	52% 1	10%
55-64	47%	40%	13%
65+	43%	36% 2	19%

% 0   20   40   60   80   100

Christianity has an important role to play in public life

Male: Agree 57%, Disagree 39%, Refused 1%, Don't know 3%

Female: Agree 58%, Disagree 36%, Don't know 6%

On balance, religion is a force for good in society

Agree 53%, Disagree 39%, Refused 1%, Don't know 7%

Source: Communicate Research/Theos (18-19 October 2006)

Religion does more harm than good – poll

82% say faith causes tension in country where two-thirds are not religious

More people in Britain think religion causes harm than believe it does good, according to a *Guardian*/ICM poll published today. It shows that an overwhelming majority see religion as a cause of division and tension – greatly outnumbering the smaller majority who also believe that it can be a force for good.

> **An overwhelming majority see religion as a cause of division and tension – greatly outnumbering the smaller majority who also believe that it can be a force for good**

The poll also reveals that non-believers outnumber believers in Britain by almost two to one. It paints a picture of a sceptical nation with massive doubts about the effect religion has on society: 82% of those questioned say they see religion as a cause of division and tension between people. Only 16% disagree. The findings are at odds with attempts by some religious leaders to define the country as one made up of many faith communities.

Most people have no personal faith, the poll shows, with only 33% of those questioned describing themselves as 'a religious person'. A clear majority, 63%, say that they are not religious – including more than half of those who describe themselves as Christian.

Older people and women are the most likely to believe in a god, with 37% of women saying they are religious, compared with 29% of men.

By Julian Glover and Alexandra Topping

The findings come at the end of a year in which multiculturalism and the role of different faiths in society has been at the heart of a divisive political debate.

But a spokesman for the Church of England denied yesterday that mainstream religion was the source of tension. He also insisted that the 'impression of secularism in this country is overrated'.

'You also have to bear in mind how society has changed. It is more difficult to go to church now than it was. Communities are displaced, people work longer hours – it's harder to fit it in. It doesn't alter the fact that the Church of England will get 1 million people in church every Sunday, which is larger than any other gathering in the country.'

The Right Rev Bishop Dunn, Bishop of Hexham and Newcastle, added: 'The perception that faith is a cause of division can often be because faith is misused for other uses and other agendas.'

The poll suggests, however, that in modern Britain religious observance has become a habit reserved for special occasions. Only 13% of those questioned claimed to visit a place of worship at least once a week, with 43% saying they never attended religious services.

Non-Christians are the most regular attendees – 29% say they attend a religious service at least weekly. Yet Christmas remains a religious festival for many people, with 54% of Christians questioned saying they intended to go to a religious service over the holiday period.

Well-off people are more likely to plan to visit a church at Christmas: 64% of those in the highest economic categories expect to attend, compared with 43% of those in the bottom group.

Britain's generally tolerant attitude to religion is underlined by the small proportion who say the country is best described as a Christian one. Only 17% think this. The clear majority, 62%, agree Britain is better described as 'a religious country of many faiths'.

ICM interviewed a random sample of 1,006 adults aged 18+ by telephone between 12 and 13 December. Interviews were conducted across the country and the results have been weighted to the profile of all adults. ICM is a member of the British Polling Council and abides by its rules.

23 December 2006

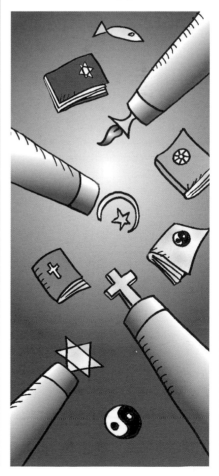

Christians feel they are discriminated against

Information from Ekklesia

A new survey carried out by the BBC has revealed that 33 per cent of Christians in the UK think that the way they are portrayed in the media amounts to discrimination. And 25% said they also experienced discrimination from colleagues in the workplace when their faith was known or talked about.

---

33 per cent of Christians in the UK think that the way they are portrayed in the media amounts to discrimination

---

The poll was carried out for the BBC's *Heaven and Earth* programme, based on a representative sample of 604 people. Another 22% said they thought Christians faced discrimination in their local community. 19 per cent said they would be passed over for promotion. A third thought the media distorted Christian issues.

Matters like the British Airways prohibition on costume jewellery, which prevented an employee from wearing a cross, and suspicion towards Christian service organisations by funding bodies, were cited as examples.

Conservative MP Anne Widdecombe, an Anglican who became a Catholic, said: 'It's now entirely a matter for Christians whether we fight back or take it. My own belief is that we should stand together and fight this discrimination.'

But the UK Christian think-tank Ekklesia, which said that the findings confirmed the discoveries of its own research over the past four years, argued that 'retreating into a persecution mentality' is bad for

Christianity and bad for society.

'Christians are also privileged – for example there are 26 unelected bishops in the house of Lords, and a quarter of state-funded primary schools are run by churches selecting on the basis of people's faith', said Ekklesia co-director Jonathan Bartley on the *Heaven and Earth Show* this morning.

He also said that when Muslims and Jews faced attacks and desecration of their cemeteries, talk of 'persecution' needed to be put into context.

'The reason a sizable minority of Christians, especially more conservative ones, are feeling "got at" is because the historic privilege and influence of the churches is being eroded in the public sphere,' commented Ekklesia co-director Simon Barrow after the show.

'But this demonstrates how easy it has been, during the era of Christendom, for Christians to mistake their own power for the gospel message – which involves Jesus embodying God's special concern for those at the margins, not demanding special treatment for religion,' he added.

Ekklesia argues that loss of automatic privileges, the challenges of pluralism in public life, and the criticism churches face over discrimination in schools and services is 'a historic opportunity for them to recover a vision of the Christian message as rooted in justice and equality. Self-interest and trying to grab power back is an unhelpful response – a counter-witness, even.'

The think-tank has also warned about the dangers of 'the politics of competitive grievance', where Christians, secularists, Muslims and others try to outdo each other with claims of discrimination, rather than looking at how to work together.

A BBC researcher on the *Heaven and Earth Show* team spoke to four other Christian agencies, which made similar claims to those demonstrated in their survey. A spokesperson for one charity in London said it was told to 'de-Christianise' if it had any chance of getting funding. Another was told it needed to take all mention of Christianity off its website; otherwise it was at risk of not receiving any money.

A Reading-based Christian homeless group also complained that it was no longer able to employ only Christians. However, Ekklesia's Jonathan Bartley said this was not discrimination, but equal opportunities which Christians, alongside others, were rightly expected to uphold when public money was involved.

And the Anglican Bishop of Bolton, David Gillett, responded: 'Religion is big news these days, so people have become more conscious of faith issues. That means Christians are now finding decisions going against them in a more high-profile way. But it's a case of those issues getting more attention, rather than there being more discrimination.'

Meanwhile former PR guru Lynne Franks told the BBC's *Heaven and Earth Show* that claims of discrimination against Christians, defended by outspoken Catholic journalist Joanna Bogle, were 'off the mark'. The National Secular Society's news monitoring service dubbed them 'crackpot' and said Christians were 'over-privileged'.
18 March 2007

⇨ The above information is reprinted with kind permission from Ekklesia. Visit www.ekklesia.co.uk for more information.

© *Ekklesia*

Religious hate crime

Information from Directgov

Crimes that are motivated by religious hatred will be treated seriously. Anyone found guilty of a religiously motivated crime will be given a more severe punishment than someone who commits the same crime without prejudice.

What is religious hate crime?

Religious hate crimes happen when someone is attacked or threatened because of their religion or their beliefs. Although racial and religious hatred may seem very similar, the police and the courts may treat racial crimes differently to religious ones.

Religion and the law

Religious hate crime is not currently recognised as a criminal offence in the same way as racial and homophobic crime.

However, if a crime is committed against someone because of their religion, it may be interpreted as an attack on their race as well. This means it can be treated as a racially aggravated or motivated attack. For example, criminal courts have decided that attacks on Sikhs and Jewish people are racial incidents.

If it's proven that the offender's main motivation was based on prejudice or their hatred of another race, then the sentence can be more severe than for the same offence without a racial motivation.

Incitement to religious hatred

It is illegal to say anything or produce any written material that tries to persuade someone to commit a criminal offence against another race or group of people. This means that leaflets, flyers or speeches that promote crime against people because of their religion are against the law. This is called incitement to religious hatred.

However, it is not against the law to disagree with or criticise someone because of their religion or their beliefs.

Reporting a religious crime

If you think you have become a victim of a crime because of your religion, then you should report it to the police as soon as possible. Whether the crime is proven to have been committed because of religious prejudice or not, it is still a crime in its own right.

You should also make sure that the incident is reported to your local Community Safety Unit. Every police force in the country has one of these units and it's their job to monitor and record the number of hate crimes that are committed in your area. They work within the community to combat the problem.

Religious discrimination at work

Discrimination law means that employers must make sure that all their employees are treated in the same way as each other, regardless of their religious beliefs.

Your local Citizens' Advice Bureau will be able to tell you the steps you should take if you have a religious discrimination case against your employer.

You could also try speaking to ACAS who provide up-to-date information, independent advice, for employees to solve problems.

↳ Information from Directgov. Visit www.direct.gov.uk for more.

New legislation to combat religious hatred

Information from Directgov

Incitement to religious hatred will today become a criminal offence in England and Wales with the commencement of the Racial and Religious Hatred Act.

The Act creates a new offence of intentionally stirring up religious hatred against people on religious grounds, closing a gap in the current legislation.

Existing offences in the Public Order Act 1986 legislate against inciting racial hatred. Jews and Sikhs have been deemed by the courts to be racial groups and are protected under this legislation, but other groups such as Muslims and Christians are considered to be religious rather than racial groups and have therefore not previously received any protection under the law.

The new Act will give protection to these groups by outlawing the use of threatening words or behaviour intended to incite hatred against groups of people defined by their religious beliefs or lack of belief.

Home Office Minister Vernon Coaker said:

'This Act closes this small but important gap in the law against extremists who stir up hatred in our communities. To be attacked or targeted because of your race or religion is wholly unacceptable.

'It can have a devastating effect on victims who can find themselves on the receiving end of bigotry and hatred.

'We are committed to protecting everyone in our society and legislating against this abhorrent behaviour. Our overarching goal is to build a civilised society where we can all achieve our potential free from prejudice.'
1 October 2007

⇨ Information from Directgov. Visit www.direct.gov.uk for more.

Extremism: the battle for young hearts and minds

Information from *Young People Now*

In the wake of the recent terrorist attacks in London and Glasgow, Tom de Castella asks whether the right measures are in place to prevent young people forming extremist views.

Two years ago this week, suicide bombs on three tube trains and a bus killed 52 people in London. And only last week further carnage was avoided when bombers narrowly failed to detonate car bombs in central London and at Glasgow Airport. Few details have emerged about the perpetrators of last week's attacks, but it is believed that like the 7/7 London bombers, they were inspired by a warped view of Islam.

The Government has admitted that police investigations can only deal with the symptoms of the problem. So last autumn it set up the Preventing Violent Extremism Team at the Home Office, which has since been moved to Communities and Local Government.

In April this year, the first work from the unit was published in its flagship report *Preventing violent extremism – Winning hearts and minds*, which set out the challenge society faces, and suggested key responses to the threat of home-grown terrorism.

Action plan

The report made clear that its focus was Britain's Muslim community, although it tried to avoid stigmatising people of that faith: 'This is not about a clash of civilisations or a struggle between Islam and "the West" … Indeed, Government is committed to working in partnership with the vast majority of Muslims who reject violence and who share core British values in doing this.'

In practical terms, the action plan pledged work with madrassahs – mosque schools attended by 100,000 children aged between five and 14 years old – to develop citizenship education. Communities and Local Government would also work more closely with Muslim organisations that firmly rejected violence and promoted shared values.

Steps would be taken to improve the governance and leadership of mosques by encouraging more faith-based organisations to register with the Charity Commission and by devising an accredited continuous professional development programme for faith leaders. A £6m Pathfinder fund was also launched to support projects in 70 priority local authority areas.

But some in the youth sector have severe misgivings about the line that Whitehall is taking. A senior figure from one of the most prominent Pathfinders criticised the Government for focusing on Muslims, which he argues threatens to further alienate young Asians fed up with being branded as untrustworthy.

So what do those people living in areas with high ethnic minority populations think? Sameer, 19, is a peer mentor at a Bradford youth project called New Neighbours. He says that since the terrorist attacks on London, life has become more difficult but there are also positive signs: 'Now I have a beard people look at me differently. There is more hostility but at the same time people smile and show respect, and there is more interest being shown in the community.'

For Sameer the big challenge is breaking down the 'ghettos' in places like Bradford and he believes that youth work has a vital role in forging bonds between different ethnic communities.

A dozen miles away in Leeds, discussing the 7/7 bombings is difficult. Two of the four bombers spent their formative years in the deprived suburb of Beeston, including the leader Mohammad Sidique Khan. Khan was even employed by Leeds Youth Service for three years and one of the young people he worked with and befriended was Shehzad Tanweer, who blew up the train at Aldgate underground station. It is painfully ironic that the project Khan was working on was called Space, whose middle letters stood for Positive Alternatives to Crime.

Hidden terror

What makes the whole subject so difficult is that Khan was by all accounts a popular youth worker who managed to build a strong rapport with young people. If the youth service was unable to identify potential terrorists in its own ranks, how can it hope to identify disillusioned young people who are attracted to Islamic extremism?

John Paxton, principal youth worker at Leeds City Council, says that when it comes to individuals with a secret life, there is little they can do: 'People were completely shocked by Khan's role in the bombings. But there was no real way of finding out his true beliefs. Khan showed no sign of this when he worked for us.'

At the same time, youth workers are angry about the way extremism is perceived to be a Muslim issue. Eren Weekes, youth manager for the area, says that this is unfair: 'Why are we just looking at the extremist views of some Muslims? The British National Party (BNP) is operating in the community so why aren't we tackling it as well?'

She believes the media onslaught is to blame and it risks alienating young Muslims: 'They're going down the street being shouted at as "Beeston bombers". They feel discriminated against by the media and sense they are being backed into a corner and so they've got to defend themselves.'

The media should be more responsible, she argues: 'If you offer a young person £200 they're going to tell you what you want to hear, not what is necessarily true. As youth workers, we're trying to build that community up again but the media are tarnishing everything.'

Others take a different view. Even before the Pathfinder fund had been set up, Birmingham City Council appointed Yousiff Meah, formerly the head of its youth service, to lead the city's approach to tackling extremism.

Meah says that while youth work has been good at tackling socio-political issues like racism and the influence of the BNP, it has never really felt comfortable addressing religion and spirituality: 'Youth work at its best is about empowering young people to take control of their lives. But perhaps in the past youth services have shied away from the spiritual.' Unlike Weekes, he believes the challenge is of a different order to that posed by the BNP: 'The question is why British people are able to be inspired to blow up their fellow citizens. But the focus shouldn't be on Muslims per se, but on the errant use of Islam.'

Sources at Communities and Local Government told *Young People Now* that because Britain faces an 'unprecedented threat' from Islamic extremism the Government has no choice but to focus on the Muslim community. The message coming out of the department is that violent extremism is not linked to deprivation but to identity. Evidence collated by the department suggests that as young people, British Muslim extremists are not in trouble with the law or excluded from school. Rather, their teenage years are marked by a crisis of identity and growing alienation – they can neither empathise with their parents' Asian values or the British identity of their

white peers. So youth work, which is often about stopping young people from 'falling out of the system', has to engage on a wider level and challenge disaffection, officials argue.

The Pathfinder programme is the Government's attempt to address this, supporting projects and forums where young people are able to feel part of something. But some young Muslims feel these projects are just a red herring, and the sense of alienation will only continue to grow, especially if the police 'harass' their community. 'Are we living in a police state?' asks one Muslim youth worker in east London. 'I've been stopped so many times but I'm used to it. Younger people might actually get pushed into an extreme belief by these tactics.'

New Neighbours

The New Neighbours project in Bradford aims to break down barriers by bringing young people from different backgrounds together. The name was chosen by the young people when they were asked to come up with a project to build community cohesion. New Neighbours uses outdoor education to inspire young people from a range of faiths to work together and bond by overcoming challenges. The project, which began in January this year and is funded by Bradford Youth Service, the city's Outward Bound Association and the participants themselves, has already run two residentials with a group from Glasgow. The young people hit it off

immediately, and found similarities between sectarian divisions in Scotland and ethnic tensions in West Yorkshire, says Mike Burtoft, outdoor education development worker at Bradford Youth Service.

Encourage cohesion

Next month young people at New Neighbours will attempt to climb Yorkshire's three peaks to raise money to pay for the Glasgow group to come down to Bradford. 'Outdoor education is fantastic for bringing young people together,' believes Burtoft. 'It places them in a shared experience with shared vulnerabilities. It may be that they are frightened of water or open spaces but they have to work together, start relying on and trusting one another. It's proven very successful here.' The residential aspect also helps them to learn about other faiths in an informal way. 'It prompts discussions that might be awkward in a classroom environment,' says Burtoft. Sameer, a youth mentor on the project, says that New Neighbours has given him some of the best experiences of his life: 'We need different communities in Bradford to mix more and this is one of the best ways of making it happen.'
4 July 2007

⇨ Reproduced from *Young People Now* magazine with the permission of the copyright owner, Haymarket Business Publications Ltd. Visit www.ypnmagazine.com for more.
© Haymarket Business Publications Ltd

Diversity and dialogue

Building better understanding between young people living in a multi-faith society

The Diversity and Dialogue report looks at how to build better understanding between young people from different faiths and backgrounds growing up in Britain today. It examines the experiences and attitudes of young people living in multi-faith environments, beginning with an analysis of interviews with 124 young people.

The report outlines the need to create more spaces where young people with different beliefs can come together and share their beliefs and points of view. It gives an overview of interfaith work already taking place in both school and youth work settings and sets out practical ideas and case studies to inspire and support the development of more dialogue projects. The report is informed by the Diversity and Dialogue project, which analysed over 100 UK initiatives already working to bring young people from different faiths and backgrounds together. Some of the most innovative examples are highlighted.

Diversity and Dialogue has worked directly with over 300 young people in the North West, South East, West Midlands and Yorkshire and the Humber. Practical projects involved young people from all of the major world faith traditions and developed different models of youth dialogue. Highlights included creating a multi-faith trail around the British Museum, linking schools to campaign on global issues and holding a youth conference to discuss multi-faith living.

Key findings: young people's views

⇨ The young people in our sample attended multi-faith schools and had opportunities to build friendships with people from a wide range of faiths and backgrounds. Almost all agreed that their experiences had led them to value diversity and get beyond stereotypes and prejudice. They appreciated the chance to learn from people with different beliefs.

⇨ Most were in favour of multi-faith education because they feared that a lack of contact would lead to misunderstanding and fear between different groups. Similarly, most felt that interfaith relations were far better in their schools than in the wider world, because outside school people were more segregated and judgemental.

⇨ In addition to personal inter-action, some acknowledged the importance of formal learning about different faiths and values, for example through Religious Education.

⇨ The (predominantly white) non-religious young people were often least comfortable discussing beliefs and values, both because they worried about causing offence to others and because they were unclear about their own beliefs and moral framework.

⇨ The young people emphasised how integrated they were in comparison to their parents' generation. However, many still felt that relations between those from different faiths and backgrounds would get worse in the future.

⇨ Many felt powerless to prevent the escalation of conflicts and prejudice, fuelled by global and political tensions. They emphasised issues such as the war in Iraq and their negative impact on community relations. The young people often mistrusted the media and government. They lacked information and space to consider complex issues.

The report has identified two key components in building a successful multi-faith society:

a) Ensuring that young people have opportunities to meet and to form constructive relationships with people from other faiths and backgrounds.

> 'The only cause of conflict is not knowing. If you're completely oblivious to other religions then you won't understand. They are going to be alien to you and you won't like them.'
> Non-religious female, aged 14
> 'If religion comes up then we debate it and talk, but then we say "Ok, you think that and I think this" but we still respect each other.'
> Sikh male, age 15
> 'There's no separation between the different religions in the school... You're not exactly a Muslim or a Christian or a Sikh child, you're just a child in the school.'
> Muslim female, aged 15

b) Developing young people's skills to share their own beliefs and values and to understand and respect those of other people.

Key findings: building understanding in schools

⇨ Schools face different challenges depending on their religious make-up and their location. Multi-faith schools automatically give opportunities for young people to build friendships across faith boundaries. However, they still need to ensure that young people understand and respect both their own and other people's beliefs.

⇨ All schools should create more spaces where students can discuss complex local, global, moral and political issues and learn to understand different religious and secular viewpoints.

⇨ Religious Education and Citizen-ship offer the most obvious spaces for discussing faith and values. However, at present the level of dialogue is often dependent on the commitment of individual teachers.

⇨ Single and majority faith schools may face challenges in providing their students with first-hand experience of different religions and in dismantling stereotypes. There can be difficulties persuading less diverse schools of the relevance of interfaith work and consequently, teachers often lack support in setting up dialogue projects.

⇨ School linking projects between schools with different religious and ethnic make-ups are still rare in England and are mainly at primary level. Linking projects can be an important first step in providing opportunities for young people from different faiths and backgrounds to meet.

Key findings: building understanding outside in the community

⇨ Youth interfaith work is still at an incipient stage, but it is attracting increasing interest and rapidly gaining momentum.

⇨ Increased government and other funding is helping to finance a growing number of projects. The National Youth Agency and other youth organisations are also pressing for a greater emphasis on social cohesion and religious sensitivity within wider youth work.

⇨ Projects that build understanding between young people from different faiths are being initiated by adult interfaith bodies as well as by youth organisations. They tend to fall into two categories:
   ↳ interfaith dialogue groups or one-off events which tend to involve articulate, motivated young people;
   ↳ social cohesion projects that often focus their work on skills-building in divided communities.

Both should be expanded and encouraged, but there is also a need for more sustained interfaith youth projects, involving a wider range of young people.

⇨ A wider range of youth organisations and public institutions should get involved with promoting positive interfaith relations. These could include museums, theatres, town halls as well as youth and community groups.

⇨ Diversity and Dialogue's practical projects have experimented with different dialogue models. They indicate that sustained youth projects need a focus. Campaigns on global issues or local social action projects can be an effective way to get young people working together. They engage young people and empower them to bring about positive change.

⇨ It is important to let young people lead their own projects. However, it is also worth taking time to build relationships with adult faith organisations, as this will help to widen the impact of projects.

Diversity and Dialogue – background

Diversity and Dialogue is a partnership project between the following organisations:

CAFOD, Christian Aid, Citizenship Foundation, Islamic Relief, the Jewish Council for Racial Equality, Muslim Aid, Oxfam, Save the Children and World Jewish Aid.

The directors of these Christian, Jewish, Muslim and secular organisations came together in July 2002 to discuss the aftermath of September 11th and ongoing conflicts in the Middle East. They were concerned about the impact that these events were having on local community relations. In response, they committed to working together on the Diversity and Dialogue project.

The premise of the project is that if young people have opportunities to form strong relationships and understand each other's beliefs, then events from elsewhere will be less likely to have a negative impact on their attitudes to one another. Therefore the project has worked in the UK to investigate ways to build better understanding among young people. It has brought young people with different beliefs together to work on constructive projects addressing local and global issues. Whilst it recognises that a wide range of factors can cause barriers to forming constructive relationships, it has focused particularly on the impact of global events and politics on local community relations.

Diversity and Dialogue has been set against a backdrop of increasing political, media and public interest in the role that religion plays in our society and our identities. This has run alongside escalating tensions between those with different beliefs at a global level. The need for dialogue and cooperation between young people from different backgrounds has become even more acute. Encouragingly, Diversity and Dialogue has found great commitment to building a successful multi-faith society among the schools, community groups, institutions and of course, young people, that we have worked with during the project.

⇨ The above information is reprinted with kind permission from the Citizenship Foundation. Visit www.diversityanddialogue.org.uk for more information.

© Citizenship Foundation

Young people and religion

Is there a need to protect the young from religion?

Geneticist and atheist Richard Dawkins has set up a Foundation for Reason and Science, which aims to promote scientific study and counter religious indoctrination in schools as well as in other areas of society. Is there a need to protect the young from religion?

YES – Andrew Copson, education officer, British Humanist Association

The most wonderful thing we can do for young people is let them explore for themselves the rich diversity of human culture. That includes educating them about religious philosophies, as well as about humanist and other secular philosophies. Unfortunately, too many religions have a tendency to deny young people access to certain knowledge or opinions. We have a duty of care not to let young people be indoctrinated in this way.

YES – Terry Sanderson, president, National Secular Society

I've been campaigning for a long time for religious education to be taken out of schools. That does not mean to say that there should be no notion of religion, but that it should be included in things like history and geography where it's relevant. It should not be a subject on its own. People who are attracted to that kind of teaching are generally enthusiasts who have to spread the word.

NO – Yvonne Criddle, national youth officer, Church of England

Religion and faith help young people, and all of us, to a greater understanding and sense of our spirit, soul and psyche. For many, religion will give a purpose and meaning to life. If we ignore the spiritual side of our humanness, how will this distort our responses to the aspects of our lives that cannot be understood through reason and logic alone? What happens to love? Our role, in working with young people, is to help them discover their full potential, including values and beliefs.

NO – Richard James, director, Oxygen, Kingston Youth for Christ

In a multicultural age, where faith plays such a prominent role, young people need to be given the chance to explore faith. As one famous scholar said, the cure for bad religion isn't no religion but good religion. Having seen the positive impact that a personal faith has had on some of the troubled young people I know, I believe faith-based youth organisations should encourage young people to wrestle with the big questions in life.

6 December 2006

⇨ Reproduced from *Young People Now* magazine with the permission of the copyright owner, Haymarket Business Publications Ltd. Visit www.ypnmagazine.com for more.

© Haymarket Business Publications Ltd

Faith schools in Britain

Arguments for

⇨ Faith schools (or church schools) are on average more successful academically; their religious ethos means every child is cared for and the school itself has a unifying set of values.

⇨ Parents have a right to educate their children in accordance with their beliefs. At faith schools, such beliefs will be respected; state schools are becoming increasingly hostile to religion.

⇨ Some inner-city church schools are extraordinarily racially diverse. They are not enclaves of white middle-class children. In Roman Catholic schools, the proportion having free school meals is about the national average.

⇨ 'Ending faith schools' really means cutting off their funding, which would lead to many of them charging fees. Then they would become more socially exclusive.

⇨ Muslim schools have to follow the national curriculum, teach respect for all faiths, and are not allowed to discriminate against females. They help integrate Muslims into the wider community.

Arguments against

⇨ British society is now essentially secular, and the state should not favour or promote any religion. Religion is the main cause of conflict in the world.

⇨ Because faith schools only educate a small proportion of children, they promote separation and division. In Northern Ireland, faith schools have been a cause of the sectarianism.

⇨ Allowing CofE and RC faith schools obliges the Government to permit Muslim schools, to avoid a charge of discrimination. More Muslim schools would increase the segregation of the community into Muslim and non-Muslim, and build walls of misunderstanding and ignorance between them.

⇨ Muslim schools could be dominated by fundamentalists, who would promote jihadism and terrorism and teach that females are second-class citizens.

⇨ The requirement for parents to display some religious involvement to qualify their children for a faith school place leads to hypocrisy, with atheist parents feeling they have to go to church on Sundays.

25 October 2006

⇨ The above information is reprinted with kind permission from the First Post. Visit www.thefirstpost.co.uk for more information.

© First Post

Faith in the education system

Information from the Department for Children, Schools and Families

Christian, Hindu, Jewish, Muslim and Sikh faith school backers today, for the first time, unveiled a joint declaration and shared vision of schools with a religious character in 21st century England.

In 'Faith in the System', the Government and religious groups providing schools 'confirm our commitment to continue to work together and with schools with and without a religious character to improve the life chances of children, to build bridges to greater mutual trust and understanding and to contribute to a just and cohesive society'.

The document also aims to dispel some of the common myths and misunderstanding around schools with a religious character and seeks to promote greater respect of the differences between different faiths and different types of schools.

Speaking at the launch event at the British Library, Children, Schools and Families Secretary Ed Balls said: 'For hundreds of years faith groups have had a long and noble tradition at the heart of our education system – from medieval times, through the Reformation, to the present day. Today, around one-third of the total schools have a religious character.

'I fully recognise that faith schools are popular with many parents and make a valuable contribution to the way in which this country educates its children.

'Faith in the System is a ground-breaking document representing the Government's and religious groups' commitment to ensuring that every child, wherever they start in life, gets to experience the best our education system has to offer.'

The Archbishop of Canterbury, Dr Rowan Williams, said: 'I very much welcome the clear commitment to the role of faith-based schools within the system of education in this country which the government is affirming. The more that religious schools form an integral part of our overall educational provision, the better the chances of educating all students sensitively in what it actually feels like to share convictions of faith.

'Church of England schools are proud of their distinctive ethos: they offer not a programme of indoctrination, but the possibility of developing a greater level of community cohesion through the understanding of how faith shapes common life. This matters for the lives of individuals, whether they are believers or not – because the failure to understand how faith operates leaves us at sea in engaging with our neighbours at local and global level.'

Cardinal Cormac Murphy-O'Connor said: 'I welcome the Government's very public recognition of the contribution made by faith schools to the harmony of our society as a whole.

'An ongoing partnership between the Catholic Church and the Government based on the right of Catholic parents – under the Human Rights Act – to choose a Catholic education for their children is a proven way of forming youngsters as good British citizens of the future.

'I welcome this Vision Statement and the support of the Government for faith communities in this educational endeavour.'

Henry Grunwald, QC, President of the Board of Deputies of British Jews, said: 'This is an important document – one that needs to be read again and again by elected officials, the media and anyone interested in the health of education in Britain. "Faith in the System" goes a long way towards dispelling the myths, preconceived notions and negative stereotypes surrounding faith schools and demonstrates their role in ensuring that British society continues to aspire to the highest ideals of toleration and mutual respect.'

Dr Mohamed Mukadam, Chairman of the Association of Muslim Schools UK, said: 'The "Faith in the System" initiative presents a historic opportunity for all faith schools to work collaboratively and help British young people develop a better and deeper understanding of God and utilise this knowledge to become successful individuals.

'Any person with a genuine interest in the well-being of our nation will see this document as a step towards creating a more cohesive society where people of all races, faiths and cultures will live together in harmony and contribute positively to the social, political and economic well-being of their country.'

Dr Indarjit Singh, Director of the Network of Sikh Organisations, said: 'We are delighted to welcome this important document emphasising the commitment of faith-based schools and government to work together to promote tolerance and understanding. Its message echoes Guru Nanak's teaching that our different religions are different paths to an understanding of God, and that all should be respected. The Gurus showed this respect by adding verses of Hindu and Muslim saints in our holy scriptures the Guru Granth Sahib. This respect for other faiths also permeates the curriculum and ethos of the first voluntary aided primary and secondary Sikh schools in Hayes. Respect is the binding force for true community cohesion and on behalf of all Sikhs we welcome this initiative.'

Nitesh Gor, Director of I-Foundation, said: 'The Hindu community is the latest entrant to state-funded faith education; as such, we have much to learn from our fellow faith education providers. Collaboration amongst the different faiths towards the Faith in the System declaration provides a firm foundation upon which new entrants like us can ensure best practice. We feel honoured to have been able to contribute to this document, and believe that this initiative indicates a bright future for faith schools in a multi-cultural, multi-faith society – and not least for the very first Hindu state-aided faith school to be launched in 2008.'

Schools with a religious character play an integral part in the publicly-funded school system and in society.

⇨ Around a third of all maintained schools have a religious character, approximately 6,850 schools from a total of nearly 21,000. Around 600 are secondary schools with the remainder being primary schools. The great majority are Church of England and Roman Catholic.

⇨ The remainder comprise 37 Jewish schools; seven Muslim schools; two Sikh schools; one Greek Orthodox and one Seventh Day Adventist school.

⇨ A further 13 faith schools have been approved to open over the next two years. They include one Jewish, three Muslim and one Sikh, two Church of England and two Church of England/Methodist.

⇨ Of the 83 Academies now open, 27 have a faith designation – 16 are non-denominational Christian, eight Church of England, two Catholic and one Anglican/Roman Catholic.

⇨ All maintained schools and Academies, including those with a religious character, must act in accordance with the Admissions Code, a system where all children, regardless of their background, have a fair opportunity of gaining a place at the school they want to attend. The law rules out interviewing and prevents the new introduction of selection by ability. Only when a faith school is oversubscribed can it start to give priority to pupils who practise their faith or denomination.

⇨ Many faith schools choose to give some of their places to children of no faith or other faiths. The Church of England has announced that at least 25 per cent of places in their new schools will be available as community places.

⇨ All future faith Academies, unless directly replacing a faith school, will give priority to at least 50 per cent of places to pupils from other faiths or no faith.

⇨ All maintained schools, including those with a religious character, must teach the National Curriculum.

⇨ Faith schools are often highly diverse. At secondary schools, 21 per cent of children in faith schools have a minority ethnic background compared to 17 per cent at schools without a religious character. At primary schools, 18 per cent of children in faith schools have a minority ethnic background compared to 24 per cent at primary schools without a religious character.

⇨ All schools now have a duty to promote community cohesion.
10 September 2007

⇨ The above information is reprinted with kind permission from the Department for Children, Schools and Families. Visit www.dcsf.gov.uk for more information.
© Crown copyright

Creationism – coming soon to a school near you?

Information from the Institute of Education

Creationism – the belief that life came into existence as described in Genesis or the Qur'an – is on the rise in the UK, making the teaching of evolution a problem in some schools. Science teachers reluctant to enter the evolution/creationism controversy are likely to avoid the subject, meaning that students could leave school ignorant of a crucial part of science.

This has long been the case in the USA, where many schools avoid teaching evolution for fear of upsetting the religious right and some states have legislated to ban evolution from the curriculum unless creationism is also taught.

A new book aims to help science teachers deal with this dilemma by showing them how to take seriously and respectfully the concerns of those who do not accept the scientific worldview while introducing them to the theory of evolution.

Teaching about Scientific Origins: Taking Account of Creationism, edited by Leslie Jones (Valdosta State University, USA) and Michael Reiss (Institute of Education, University of London) is written for science teachers who want their students to understand the scientific position on the origins of the universe and life on earth. Authors explore the controversy from a variety of perspectives and suggest ways of presenting the science in a way that is true to itself while ensuring that religious students do not feel threatened.

Professor Reiss, who has a PhD in evolutionary biology and is also a priest of the Church of England, says: 'The days have long gone when science teachers could ignore creationism when teaching about origins. While it is unlikely that they will help students who have a conflict between science and their religious beliefs to resolve the conflict, good science teaching can help them to manage it – and to learn more science.

'By not dismissing their beliefs, we can ensure that these students learn what evolutionary theory really says – and give everyone the understanding to respect the views of others.'

Teaching about Scientific Origins: Taking Account of Creationism is published by Peter Lang, New York.
5 October 2007

⇨ Information from the Institute of Education, University of London. Visit www.ioe.ac.uk for more information.

© University of London

Sneaking God into science by the back door

Time for the UK to confront 'Intelligent Design'

By Elanor Taylor

In February 2006, the BBC television programme *Horizon* commissioned a MORI poll to ascertain UK public opinion on the theory of evolution. A group of over 2,000 participants were asked what best described their view of the origin and development of life, from a list including creationism, intelligent design and evolutionary theory.

⇨ 22% chose creationism;
⇨ 17% opted for intelligent design;
⇨ 48% selected evolutionary theory;
⇨ the rest didn't know.

According to this poll, just over half of the British public are not convinced by evolutionary theory. Even given caveats about the validity of polls as a way of measuring public opinion, these are worrying statistics.

Creationism and its newer, shinier offshoot, intelligent design, have up until recently been regarded in the UK as peculiarly American phenomena. Interesting debates perhaps, especially the recent school curriculum cases in Ohio and Kansas but, like line-dancing and SUVs, not the sort of things to ever cause problems in Britain.

The *Horizon* poll, along with some other recent developments, would suggest otherwise. In February 2006, the *Guardian* reported that creationism and support for intelligent design was worryingly on the rise in the UK student population. Geneticist Steve Jones described this as 'an insidious and growing problem', and has been commissioned by the Royal Society to give a talk in April with the unambiguous title 'Why Creationism is Wrong'. More extremely, creationism is taught quite openly in biology classes as an alternative to Darwin in the trio of Vardy Foundation schools in the north of England, which are controversially funded by a local evangelical Christian businessman.

So, just as line-dancing classes are now a staple at the local community centre, and the south of England gets increasingly clogged up with SUVs, it looks like creationism and intelligent design may also be added to the list of unlikely US exports that have taken root in the UK.

Creationism and intelligent design

For some, there is a feeling that we have been here before. Didn't we go through all of this with creationism decades ago? Haven't we dealt with all of this stuff already? The answer is yes and no. While creationism and intelligent design come from the same place – a belief that the universe and everything in it was designed – intelligent design has been presented as a 'scientific' position, and this has changed the overall nature of the debate.

Creationism is a position based on the Bible. Creationists generally believe that God created the universe in 6 days because the Bible tells us so. This entails a flat denial of Darwinian evolution, and often also comes in conjunction with 'young-earth-ism', the belief that the scientific estimates about the age of the earth are secondary to Bible accounts. Creationism is now thought to be mostly the preserve of evangelicals and extremists, although some polls in the US would suggest otherwise. The current debate is framed in terms of 'intelligent design', an idea which, although just as fundamentally religious as creationism, claims to be a scientific position rather than a religious one.

In the words of the intelligent design think tank the Discovery Institute, the ID position is:

'Certain features of the universe and of living things are best explained by an intelligent cause, not an undirected process such as natural selection.'

These 'certain features' are very complex systems. ID's most prominent defenders claim support from scientific work in biology and biochemistry, arguing that science has revealed some incredibly complex natural systems, systems which they argue are too complex to have evolved. In ID jargon, such systems are described as 'irreducibly complex'. ID proponents hold that design is a better explanation than evolution for cases of such 'irreducible complexity'.

> ## Just over half of the British public are not convinced by evolutionary theory

What ID doesn't say is almost as interesting as what ID does say. The movement has selected its proponents well – they tend to be academic scientists rather than pastors and many have PhDs from prestigious institutions. Their claim is that an intelligent designer is the best explanation of some complex natural phenomena, but the status of the designer is somewhat coyly left undeclared. As Michael Behe, one of ID's most prolific and vocal supporters, said in a recent interview with the *Guardian*:

'All that the evidence from biochemistry points to is some very intelligent agent. Although I find it congenial to think that it's God, others might prefer to think it's an alien – or who knows? An angel, or some satanic force, some new age power. Something we don't know about yet.'

Their argument is that support for intelligent design comes from science, not from religion. ID proponents tend to keep their mouths closed about their religious beliefs in public, claiming that they have been led towards intelligent design out of a thirst for adequate explanation rather than religious preoccupations. However, after a first glance, and after wading through the mass of scientific jargon in pro-ID material like Behe's book *Darwin's Black Box*, or any of the innumerable ID blogs out there, one thing becomes clear – intelligent design is a religious position, not a scientific one. By attempting to frame this argument in terms of science, the intelligent design movement are seriously misrepresenting their own position in an attempt to garner popular and political support for their agenda.

Scientific problems

Going a little deeper into intelligent design claims shows that its claims to scientific validity are unwarranted. First of all there is the general point about peer review – no research in support of ID has ever been published in a peer-reviewed journal. This in itself should indicate problems with a position and a research programme with a supposedly respectable scientific basis. But for those who would demand more detail on the problems with intelligent design, we need only look to the work of one of ID's most high-profile supporters, Michael Behe.

Behe is a professor of biochemistry at the University of Lehigh in Bethlehem, Pennsylvania. His arguments are mostly based on biochemistry, and he is credited with bringing the notion of 'irreducible complexity' into common usage in his 1998 work *Darwin's Black Box*, which makes the case for intelligent design against Darwinian evolution as explanation of complex natural phenomena. To a non-scientist some of the biochemical detail in Behe's book is daunting, but his argument boils down to the position that there are certain systems in nature which have many parts, and which require the operation of all of their parts to work. As he puts it:

'By irreducibly complex I mean a single system composed of several well-matched interacting parts that contribute to the basic function, wherein the removal of any one of the parts causes the system to effectively cease functioning.'

The given examples of irreducibly complex systems range from blood-clotting to mouse-traps.

Behe holds that no scientist has ever shown how an irreducibly complex system might have evolved. This leads him to hold that gradualist explanations, whereby a system would develop in complexity gradually over generations, cannot explain these particular phenomena. Behe then argues that the inference to design is the best way of explaining the supposedly sudden appearance of such extremely complicated systems.

Biochemists' responses to this argument are unambiguous – irreducible complexity is not a problem for evolutionary biology, and such systems can be shown to have evolved. Professor P.Z. Myers, Professor of Biology at the University of Minnesota and ardent pro-evolutionary blogger, makes the following point about Behe's claims:

'"Irreducible complexity" is one of those things the ID people have gotten a lot mileage from, but every competent biologist immediately recognises its antecedents: Muller's ratchet. Muller made the argument back around 1925 that genetic processes would naturally lead to increasing complexity; cycles of gene duplication and addition to pathways would unavoidably lead to more and more steps. Contrary to Behe, the phenomenon he describes is actually a prediction of 80-year-old genetics.'

Myers' rebuttal of Behe's position on irreducible complexity can be found here, as can some more material about evolutionary approaches to irreducible complexity.

In the recent Dover trial in Ohio, where the local school board's decision to teach intelligent design as an alternative to evolution in biology classes was overturned, Judge Jones made the following statement about irreducible complexity:

'The argument of irreducible complexity, central to ID, involves the same flawed and illogical contrived dualism that doomed creation science in the 1980s.'

Some are worried that Intelligent Design is in reality another form of Creationism – for Christians, the belief that the origins of humankind are literally as described in Genesis

The decision was influenced by expert testimony, details of which can be found in the full text of the decision. It is clear that scientific opinion is against Behe on this point. Irreducible complexity is an insufficient basis for any scientific position, and cannot support the weight of intelligent design.

Conceptual problems

However, it is unnecessary to take intelligent design in terms of science to see the flaws in pro-ID arguments. If irreducible complexity is not a problem for evolutionary biology then it is clearly important to point this out, but as a non-scientist I would argue that we don't need the evidence of chemistry or biology to see the flaws in the pro-ID position.

The inference to design is only ever an inference to the best explanation from a religious perspective. For those who don't have a particular religious agenda, it is natural to want to exhaust other avenues of enquiry before positing supernatural beings to explain our scientific problems. The intelligent design movement, for all of its claims about scientific evidence pointing towards design, has to go through some ridiculous intellectual contortions in order to wedge the idea of a designer into a genuinely scientific worldview.

Intelligent design makes no room for the idea of bad design, and irreducible complexity itself suggests a bad design strategy. Making complex things all at once so that they only work if all of the components are present and fully operational is an inefficient way to put something together. Are we to assume that not only is this intelligent designer mysterious, but also that he, she or it is perhaps a bit rubbish? The best explanation of complex systems in nature, which encompasses all of the bits that do 'work' and all of the bits that don't, is that they evolved. Positing a designer with their own private reasons for designing things badly is simply a step too far in what is claimed to be a scientifically grounded inference to the best explanation.

As new areas of science grow and develop, areas appear which require research, where questions have not yet been fully answered. Intelligent design is jumping on these areas, and taking the inability of evolutionary scientists to offer a complete explanation of some very specific cases as evidence that evolution is completely wrong. As Richard Dawkins puts it:

'If the scientists fail to give an immediate and comprehensive answer, a default conclusion is drawn: "Right then, the alternative theory, intelligent design, wins by default."'

Without any scientific backing of their own, intelligent design proponents pounce on gaps in other scientific accounts and adopt them as support for ID. In this way, intelligent design has become a scientific parasite, seeking out academic blind spots as a way of bolstering its own strength. This can only be bad for scientific progress, as the unanswered questions that science thrives on are continually held up as evidence of the failure of evolutionary theory, and in favour of a mysterious designer.

A problem for the UK?

The recent educational cases in Ohio and Kansas were watched with great interest from this side of the Atlantic. However, it may be time to take some lessons from the US cases as well as news material if intelligent design is to be prevented from becoming a major problem in the UK.

One of the interesting features of the intelligent design debate in the

US was the initial unwillingness of the scientific authorities to engage in debate on the issue. Intelligent design, as an offshoot of creationism, was seen to be self-evidently dodgy. Scientists didn't want to dignify it by speaking out against it. This is an understandable tactic which eventually backfired, allowing the intelligent design factions to take a 'what are they scared of?' approach.

Intelligent design is now a coherent movement with vocal, well-educated proponents, extensive literature, substantial funding and a relentlessly enthusiastic online supporters' community. It is therefore an issue which cannot be ignored. The American Association for the Advancement of Science has now responded to the intelligent design challenge well, with an extensive public information campaign, lectures and online resources. A pro-evolution blogging community has also taken up the online challenge, with lively and articulate results.

One major problem for the issue of schools teaching is that the call to 'teach the controversy', to teach both evolution and some form of ID in classrooms, sounds at first to be an open-minded position. Teaching the controversy sounds like a sensible thing to do, if there are genuinely two alternative scientific theories. But ID is not a genuine alternative to evolution, as it has no scientific backing, so teaching the controversy is misleading rather than fair-minded. It is therefore of the utmost importance to get the idea that ID is not a valid alternative across, so as to avoid the school science teaching fiascos we have witnessed in the US.

Stalwart defenders of evolution Richard Dawkins and Daniel Dennett are, as always, responding to the challenge well. The Royal Society is also hosting the aforementioned public talk by geneticist Stephen Jones. Thousands of members of religious communities across the globe have signed up to the Clergy Letter Project, an open letter which maintains that:

'The theory of evolution is a foundational scientific truth, one that has stood up to rigorous scrutiny and upon which much of human

knowledge and achievement rests. To reject this truth or to treat it as "one theory among others" is to deliberately embrace scientific ignorance and transmit such ignorance to our children.'

All of this effort is immensely valuable, but it will have to be sustained to be effective. The most important lesson the UK can take from

the recent US schools cases is that intelligent design cannot be ignored. By going out to bat for evolution, by continually publicly emphasising the illegitimacy of intelligent design as an alternative to evolutionary theory, UK scientists, teachers, writers and learned institutions can all work together to ensure that intelligent design does not become a problem for the UK. Information is the only weapon against ignorance. Making a loud noise about evolution will therefore be the best way to prevent intelligent design from bringing God into science through the back door.
16 March 2006

⇨ Information from the Social Issues Research Centre. Visit www.sirc.org for more information.
© Social Issues Research Centre

KEY FACTS

⇨ Many religions offer their followers answers to philosophical questions about topics such as how and why the universe came into existence, the purpose of life and the best way to live it, and what happens after death. (page 1)

⇨ Buddhism is more than 2,500 years old and has more than 2,000 sects. It developed in North India in the 6th or 5th century BC, when Siddhartha Gautama attained 'enlightenment' – the ultimate truth by which people are freed from the cycle of re-birth. (page 2)

⇨ The term 'Hinduism' is used to describe the ancient religious culture of India. This culture is over 5,000 years old and is practised by countless millions. Hinduism has neither a single founder, nor a single scripture that is uniquely authoritative. (page 2)

⇨ Judaism originated in the Middle East and is based on the belief in one God. According to Torah, the central scripture for Jews, God is holy and unmitigated. He is omnipotent, omniscient and eternal. (page 4)

⇨ Sikhism is a monotheistic faith, which was founded in the fifteenth century by Guru Nanak in the region of Punjab, north-west India. It is recognised as the youngest of world religions. (page 5)

⇨ 36% of young adults (18 to 34 years of age) define themselves as Atheist or Agnostic, according to a 2005 Ipsos MORI poll. (page 8)

⇨ 62% of people surveyed by Ipsos MORI in 2006 believe that human nature by itself gives us an understanding of what is right and wrong, whereas 27% believe that people need religious teachings in order to understand what is right and wrong. (page 9)

⇨ 33% of people in Britain feel that religion is important. (page 10)

⇨ Morality, ethics, values, rights, duties are all words used when people talk about issues of right and wrong, of what we ought and ought not to do. (page 16)

⇨ An overwhelming number of people believe that Britain is experiencing a moral decline according to a BBC/ComRes opinion poll. (page 17)

⇨ If both parents attend church services or at least identify with a religion, then there's a virtually 50/50 likelihood of their children doing so too. If only one of the parents attends, the likelihood is halved to 25%, and if neither of the parents attends or 'belongs', the chances of the children doing so are negligible. (page 18)

⇨ One in seven adults in the UK attends a Christian church each month, with nearly 3 million more people saying they would attend church if only they were asked, one of the largest surveys of churchgoing in the UK reveals. (page 20)

⇨ The Church of England became the established church of the land after the 16th century Reformation when Henry VIII broke ties with the Pope in Rome so he could divorce his first wife. (page 21)

⇨ Fewer than one in six of all infants is now baptised and in major cities the number has fallen to one in ten. (page 22)

⇨ 32% of people surveyed by YouGov said they were Christian, but only attended church for special services such as weddings, funerals and Christmas. (page 23)

⇨ 72% of Britain's population consider themselves Christian. However, 48% do not understand that Easter marks the death and resurrection of Jesus. (page 25)

⇨ In a survey for Theos, 57% of men and 58% of women agreed that Christianity has an important role in public life. (page 26)

⇨ In a survey for Theos, 53% of people agreed that on balance, religion is a force for good in society. (page 26)

⇨ 82% of those questioned in a *Guardian*/ICM poll say they see religion as a cause of division and tension between people. (page 27)

⇨ A new survey carried out by the BBC has revealed that 33% of Christians in the UK think that the way they are portrayed in the media amounts to discrimination. (page 28)

⇨ Religious hate crimes happen when someone is attacked or threatened because of their religion or their beliefs. Although racial and religious hatred may seem very similar, the police and the courts may treat racial crimes differently to religious ones. (page 29)

⇨ Around a third of all maintained schools have a religious character, approximately 6,850 schools from a total of nearly 21,000. Around 600 are secondary schools with the remainder being primary schools. The great majority are Church of England and Roman Catholic. (page 36)

⇨ Creationism – the belief that life came into existence as described in Genesis or the Qur'an – is on the rise in the UK, making the teaching of evolution a problem in some schools. (page 36)

GLOSSARY

Agnosticism
An agnostic believes that it is impossible to know or prove whether there is a god. The term agnostic is also used for those who are sceptical of the existence of a god, but do not firmly commit to atheism.

Atheism
Atheism refers to the firm belief that there is no god or divine power at work in the universe, and human beings are constrained to one life only, with no continued existence after death.

Christianity
Christianity is the largest religion in the world, and the state religion of the UK. Christians follow the teachings of Jesus Christ, who they believe to be the son of God, as given in the Bible – however, there are many different denominations and sects, with varying beliefs and rituals. These include Catholicism, Orthodox Christianity and Protestantism (which incorporates other groups such as the Methodists, the Baptists and the Church of England). Because of differences in their beliefs and practices, these groups will sometimes be mistakenly described as separate religions, but this is not the case: they are all denominations of Christianity.

The Golden Rule
This refers to the one idea which is common to practically all world religions and philosophies, including Humanism. Although it is phrased in different ways in the major texts of the different ideologies, the general sense of the Golden Rule is that human beings should treat other people in the same way that they themselves would wish to be treated.

Humanism
Humanism is a non-religious movement whose adherents propound an approach to life based on humanity and reason. They believe that concepts of right and wrong are derived from human nature and experience, and that we do not need religious guidance to help in making moral choices.

Islam
Islam is the second most popular religion in the UK today, as well as the fastest growing. Followers of Islam are called Muslims, and believe in the word of Allah (God) as set out in their holy book, the Qu'ran, by the prophet Muhammed in Arabia 1,300 years ago. Islam is very much a way of life as well as a religion, and followers observe strict rules regarding diet, dress and worship.

Life after death
The belief in another life following our earthly existence is fundamental to all of the major world religions, but each have different beliefs. Buddhists, Hindus and Sikhs all believe in reincarnation, a cycle of rebirth into different lives. Muslims, Jews and Christians (together known as the Abrahamic religions) all believe in the concepts of heaven and hell, where the virtuous will be rewarded and the wicked punished respectively after the death of their earthly bodies. Atheists and humanists do not believe in any form of life after death, and so believe we should make the most of our time on earth, as it is the only life we have.

Religion
The word religion comes from the Latin *religio*, which means 'duty'. It can be defined as a set of beliefs, rituals and values centred around faith in a supernatural power at work in the universe. Major world religions followed in the UK today include Christianity, Islam, Judaism, Sikhism, Hinduism and Buddhism.

Spirituality
This is related to but separate from religion. Religious believers will be spiritual people, but it is possible to be spiritual without being religious. Spirituality is a belief in each person's spirit or soul as distinct from their body, and a desire to nurture and develop one's own soul. For example, someone may believe in the value of yoga and meditation without also belonging to an organised faith.

State religion
A state religion is one which has been legally endorsed as the official faith of a country or state. The state religion of England is the Church of England (or Anglican Church), a form of Protestant Christianity. This has the monarch as its head, and the Archbishop of Canterbury as senior bishop. Some question whether the Church of England still has any relevance as the state religion in a country where only a minority still attend churches regularly.

Theism
This refers to belief in a god or gods. Other words containing the *the* affix will also relate to this topic: for example *the*ology (the study of gods and religion), mono*the*ism (the belief in one god only), poly*the*ism (the belief in several gods), a*the*ism (the belief that there is no god).

Worship
Worship of a deity or deities is central to most organised religions. This will usually take place in a sacred building such as a church, mosque or temple, where followers of a religion can gather to show their devotion to god(s) through actions such as prayer, chanting and singing, reading from a holy text and other rituals. Members of a religion will usually be led in worship by someone with special authority to do so, such as a priest or imam.

INDEX

Additional Resources

Other Issues titles

If you are interested in researching further some of the issues raised in *Religious Beliefs*, you may like to read the following titles in the **Issues** series:

➪ Vol. 150 *Migration and Population* (ISBN 978 1 86168 423 3)

➪ Vol. 147 *The Terrorism Problem* (ISBN 978 1 86168 420 2)

➪ Vol. 139 *The Education Problem* (ISBN 978 1 86168 391 5)

➪ Vol. 131 *Citizenship and National Identity* (ISBN 978 1 86168 377 9)

➪ Vol. 121 *The Censorship Debate* (ISBN 978 1 86168 354 0)

➪ Vol. 120 *The Human Rights Issue* (ISBN 978 1 86168 353 3)

➪ Vol. 116 *Grief and Loss* (ISBN 978 1 86168 349 6)

➪ Vol. 115 *Racial Discrimination* (ISBN 978 1 86168 348 9)

➪ Vol. 106 *Trends in Marriage* (ISBN 978 1 86168 326 7)

For more information about these titles, visit our website at www.independence.co.uk/publicationslist

Useful organisations

You may find the websites of the following organisations useful for further research:

➪ **About:** www.about.com

➪ **British Humanist Association:** www.humanism. org.uk

➪ **Citizenship Foundation:** www.diversityanddialogue. org.uk

➪ **Department for Children, Schools and Families:** www.dcsf.gov.uk

➪ **DirectGov:** www.direct.gov.uk

➪ **Economic and Social Research Council:** www.esrc. ac.uk

➪ **Ekklesia:** www.ekklesia.co.uk

➪ **Institute of Education:** www.ioe.ac.uk

➪ **Religious Tolerance:** www.religioustolerance.org

➪ **Social Issues Research Centre:** www.sirc.org

➪ **Tearfund:** www.tearfund.org

➪ **University of Manchester:** www.manchester.ac.uk

➪ **YouGov:** www.yougov.com

➪ **Young People Now:** www.ypnmagazine.com

ACKNOWLEDGEMENTS

The publisher is grateful for permission to reproduce the following material.

While every care has been taken to trace and acknowledge copyright, the publisher tenders its apology for any accidental infringement or where copyright has proved untraceable. The publisher would be pleased to come to a suitable arrangement in any such case with the rightful owner.

Chapter One: Religious Diversity

What is religion?, © Channel 4, *Major religions in the UK*, © University of Manchester, *Religion in Britain, and in the rest of the UK* © Religious Tolerance, *The Golden Rule*, © British Humanist Association, *Food culture and religion*, © Better Health Channel, *Why does religion exist?*, © About.com, *A humanist discussion of ethics*, © British Humanist Association, *Religion and moral decline*, © Ekklesia, *Crisis of faith?*, © Economic and Social Research Council, *One in seven adults attends church every month*, © Tearfund, *Church of England still valid as state religion?*, © Reuters, *Only one in six children is now baptised*, © Associated Newspapers Ltd.

Chapter Two: Religious Tolerance

Religion: who needs it?, © New Statesman, *Majority views religion as force for good*, © Telegraph Group Ltd, *Religion does more harm than good – poll*, © Guardian Newspapers Ltd, *Christians feel they are discriminated against*, © Ekklesia, *Religious hate crime*, © Crown copyright is reproduced with the permission of Her Majesty's Stationery Office, *New legislation to combat religious hatred*, © Crown copyright is reproduced with the permission of Her Majesty's Stationery Office, *Extremism: the battle for young hearts and minds*, © Haymarket Business Publications Ltd, *Diversity and dialogue*, © Citizenship Foundation, *Young people and religion*, © Haymarket Business Publications Ltd, *Faith schools in Britain*, © First Post, *Faith in the education system*, © Crown copyright is reproduced with the permission of Her Majesty's Stationery Office, *Creationism – coming soon to a school near you?*, © University of London, *Sneaking God into science by the back door*, © Social Issues Research Centre.

Photographs

Flickr: pages 3 (Ian); 17 (Mark Probst); 19 (Martin Gommel).
Stock Xchng: pages 15 (BSK); 22 (Sanja Gjenero); 24 (Sachin Ghodke).
Wikimedia Commons: page 38 (photograph by Yuval Madar; painting by Tiziano Vecelli [Titian]).

Illustrations

Pages 5, 12: Simon Kneebone; pages 11, 31: Don Hatcher; pages 20, 33: Angelo Madrid; pages 27, 39: Bev Aisbett.

Research by Claire Owen, with additional by Lisa Firth, on behalf of Independence Educational Publishers.

Additional editorial by Claire Owen, on behalf of Independence Educational Publishers.

And with thanks to the team: Mary Chapman, Sandra Dennis, Claire Owen and Jan Sunderland.

Lisa Firth
Cambridge
January, 2008

The Education Problem

KT-449-502

ISSUES

Volume 139

Series Editor

Lisa Firth

Independence

Educational Publishers
Cambridge

First published by Independence
PO Box 295
Cambridge CB1 3XP
England

British Library Cataloguing in Publication Data
The Education Problem – (Issues Series)
I. Firth, Lisa II. Series
379.4'1

ISBN 978 1 86168 391 5

Printed in Great Britain
MWL Print Group Ltd

Cover
The illustration on the front cover is by
Simon Kneebone.

CONTENTS

Chapter One: School Matters

Chapter Two: Higher Education

Introduction

The Education Problem is the one hundred and thirty-ninth volume in the **Issues** series. The aim of this series is to offer up-to-date information about important issues in our world.

The Education Problem looks at school matters and higher education.

The information comes from a wide variety of sources and includes:
Government reports and statistics
Newspaper reports and features
Magazine articles and surveys
Website material
Literature from lobby groups
and charitable organisations.

It is hoped that, as you read about the many aspects of the issues explored in this book, you will critically evaluate the information presented. It is important that you decide whether you are being presented with facts or opinions. Does the writer give a biased or an unbiased report? If an opinion is being expressed, do you agree with the writer?

The Education Problem offers a useful starting-point for those who need convenient access to information about the many issues involved. However, it is only a starting-point. Following each article is a URL to the relevant organisation's website, which you may wish to visit for further information.

* * * * *

Education in the UK

Information from the Economic and Social Research Council

This article provides a statistical overview of education in the UK. It is designed to introduce the topic rather than be a comprehensive summary.

Other factsheets in this series may be of interest, including *Home Learning*, *The Knowledge Economy* and *Skills*.

Schools and pupils

In the UK in 2004/5 there were 9,963,000 school pupils. Public sector schools were attended by 92 per cent (9.2 million) of pupils, while seven per cent attended one of the 2,500 non-maintained mainstream schools. One per cent of pupils attended one of the 1,400 special schools. 44 per cent of public sector pupils were in secondary schools, 55 per cent in primary schools and one per cent in nursery schools.

There are around 34,400 schools in the UK. The smallest school is Holy Island school, Northumbria, which has five pupils.

There were over half a million (560,700) teachers in public sector schools in 2002/3, with 82 per cent (457,200) of teachers in England alone. The UK average of pupils per teacher is 17.6.

The average class size in 2004/5 was 25 pupils for key stage 1, 27 pupils for key stage 2 and 22 pupils for key stages 3 and 4 (secondary school).

Costs and benefits of education

In 2003, the UK spent 5.4 per cent of Gross Domestic Product (GDP) on education (all levels), up from 5.3 per cent in 2002. The average for an OECD country is 5.5 per cent, Denmark spend 8.3 per cent of GDP on education and 3.7 per cent was spent in Turkey and Japan.

The graph 'Expenditure of GDP on education, 2003' on page three shows an international comparison of expenditure on education.

The proportion of GDP spent on education in the UK has changed little over the last decade. In 1993 it was 5.55 per cent and in 2003 it was 5.3 per cent of GDP.

Education has a positive effect on earnings. Men with a degree or equivalent earn an average of £726 per week compared to £506 for men with no qualifications. Women with a degree or equivalent earn an average of £561 per week compared to £397 for those with no qualifications. So persons qualified to degree level earn an average of 29 per cent more than those with no qualifications.

Education can be considered an investment both by the individual (e.g. tuition fees) and society (e.g. teachers' costs and reduced taxes), as there is an expectation that in the future there will be financial and economic benefits or returns. These future benefits are measured as a percentage, relative to the initial investment in education and called the rate of return (RoR). The UK has a high rate of return at around 21 per cent for degree-level educated persons. France, Sweden, Denmark and the Netherlands have rates of return from 10-15 per cent and Italy has a rate of return around 7.5 per cent.

Going to school

The school leaving age in the United Kingdom is 16, although around 73 per cent of post-compulsory education students in England stay on in further education. In the early twentieth century many children left school at age 12. In 1921 the compulsory school leaving age was set at 14; it was raised to 15 in 1947 and again to 16 in 1972. Children in Guernsey can leave school aged 15. The graph 'School entry and leaving age in EU and G8 nations' on page three shows the comparative school entry and leaving ages for the EU and G8 nations.

Since 1988, the subjects taught in state sector schools in England and Wales have been prescribed as part of the National Curriculum. This is divided into four stages: key stages (KS) one and two relate to primary

schools, whereas three and four are for secondary schools. Subjects compulsory in KS1/2 are English, mathematics, science, design and technology, history, geography, art and design, music, information and communications technology and physical education. At KS3 these same subjects are compulsory, as are a modern foreign language and citizenship. At KS4, history, geography, art and design, music and modern foreign languages become optional.

Unauthorised absence from school (truancy) is more common in Scotland than in Wales and more common in Wales than in England. In England, 1.22 per cent of all pupil half-days were missed due to unauthorised absence in secondary schools in 2005/6. For Wales, the equivalent figure was 1.7 per cent in 2004/5 and in Scotland two per cent of school half-days were lost in secondary schools due to unauthorised absences. Overall secondary schools record more unauthorised absences than primary schools. A MORI poll of nearly 5,000 pupils for the *Independent* newspaper reported that 26 per cent of pupils admitted to skipping school.

Achievement

Females out-perform males at every level of the education system. In England, girls did better overall in National Curriculum assessments at age seven (KS1), age 11(KS2) and at age 14 (KS3). Girls have a higher pass rate at GCSEs and A-levels. 58 per cent of all higher education qualifications were awarded to women.

The graph 'GCSE, SCE/NQ qualifications obtained 1996-2005' on page three shows qualifications obtained by pupils in their last year of compulsory education. Over half of all pupils (57 per cent) in their final year of compulsory education achieved the equivalent of five GCSEs grades A*-C in 2004/5. Only three per cent of pupils achieved no qualifications. The graph clearly shows a trend for more pupils to gain five or more GCSE grades A*-C. This can be viewed as an improvement in education but some commentators suggest the rise is due to examinations becoming easier or marking standards declining.

International comparisons between pupils are fundamentally hard due to countries using varied and unique assessment models. The OECD set out to standardise international assessments so international comparisons can be made. The Programme for International Student Assessment (PISA) was first conducted in 2000 and is repeated every three years. PISA was repeated in 2003, but the UK was not included in the comparison since the response rate from schools was too low to provide statistically robust and non-biased results. Furthermore, at the time of writing the 2006 results have yet to be published, so for a UK comparison data has to be taken from PISA 2000.

The participation rates for 16-year-olds who continue in post-compulsory education and training is 73 per cent

---

PISA compared pupils at age 15 across 32 countries. Pupils were assessed on their reading, mathematical and scientific abilities. The UK was ranked seventh overall in terms of average pupil score for reading, eighth for mathematics and fourth for science.

Post-compulsory education

In 2004/5 there were over 2.4 million students in further education (FE) and over 2.2 million in higher education (HE) in the UK. Of the higher education students, 530 thousand were postgraduates and 1.7 million were undergraduates. 4.4 per cent of higer education students were from EU countries and 9.5 per cent were from non-EU countries.

The participation rates for 16-year-olds who continue in post-compulsory education and training is 73 per cent. This number is made up of 78 per cent females and 68 per cent males.

Participation rates vary considerably by social class. 44 per cent of 18-year-olds in England whose parents were in higher professional occupations in 2004 were studying for a degree or equivalent compared with 13 per cent whose parents were in routine occupations. The table 'Total UCAS acceptances by socio-economic class and country 2005' on page three shows the number of persons accepted onto higher education courses in 2005 through the Universities and College Admissions Service. This shows that fewer people participate in higher education if they are from a lower routine occupation background.

There are tens of thousands of first degree courses on offer at UK universities, ranging from Accountancy (826 courses) to Zoology (123 courses). Some of the more unusual offerings include Surf & Beach Management (Swansea Institute of Higher Education), Horticulture – Golf Course Management (Harper Adams University College), Tourism and Astronomy (University of Hertfordshire) and War Studies with Theology and Religious Studies (King's College).

⇨ The above information is reprinted with kind permission from the Economic and Social Research Council. Visit www.esrc.ac.uk for more information.

© ESRC

Statistics taken from the ESRC factsheet 'Education in the UK'

Expenditure of GDP on education, 2003

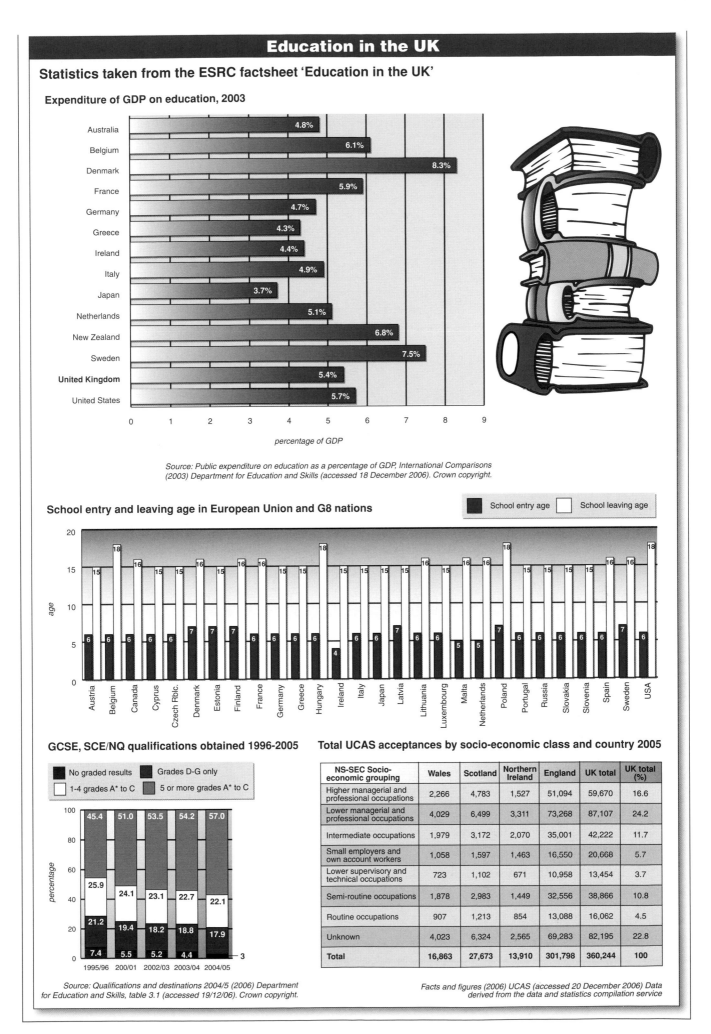

Country	percentage of GDP
Australia	4.8%
Belgium	6.1%
Denmark	8.3%
France	5.9%
Germany	4.7%
Greece	4.3%
Ireland	4.4%
Italy	4.9%
Japan	3.7%
Netherlands	5.1%
New Zealand	6.8%
Sweden	7.5%
United Kingdom	5.4%
United States	5.7%

percentage of GDP

Source: Public expenditure on education as a percentage of GDP, International Comparisons (2003) Department for Education and Skills (accessed 18 December 2006). Crown copyright.

School entry and leaving age in European Union and G8 nations

■ School entry age □ School leaving age

GCSE, SCE/NQ qualifications obtained 1996-2005

■ No graded results ■ Grades D-G only
□ 1-4 grades A* to C ▨ 5 or more grades A* to C

	1995/96	200/01	2002/03	2003/04	2004/05
5 or more grades A* to C	45.4	51.0	53.5	54.2	57.0
1-4 grades A* to C	25.9	24.1	23.1	22.7	22.1
Grades D-G only	21.2	19.4	18.2	18.8	17.9
No graded results	7.4	5.5	5.2	4.4	3

Source: Qualifications and destinations 2004/5 (2006) Department for Education and Skills, table 3.1 (accessed 19/12/06). Crown copyright.

Total UCAS acceptances by socio-economic class and country 2005

NS-SEC Socio-economic grouping	Wales	Scotland	Northern Ireland	England	UK total	UK total (%)
Higher managerial and professional occupations	2,266	4,783	1,527	51,094	59,670	16.6
Lower managerial and professional occupations	4,029	6,499	3,311	73,268	87,107	24.2
Intermediate occupations	1,979	3,172	2,070	35,001	42,222	11.7
Small employers and own account workers	1,058	1,597	1,463	16,550	20,668	5.7
Lower supervisory and technical occupations	723	1,102	671	10,958	13,454	3.7
Semi-routine occupations	1,878	2,983	1,449	32,556	38,866	10.8
Routine occupations	907	1,213	854	13,088	16,062	4.5
Unknown	4,023	6,324	2,565	69,283	82,195	22.8
Total	**16,863**	**27,673**	**13,910**	**301,798**	**360,244**	**100**

Facts and figures (2006) UCAS (accessed 20 December 2006) Data derived from the data and statistics compilation service

Qualifications explained

Do you know your AS from your GNVQ? You will now, with TheSite's quick guide to the main qualifications in the UK

GCSEs (General Certificate of Secondary Education)

These are studied during Years 10 and 11 and generally sat in Year 11 of school; however, school leavers of any age can also choose to study GCSEs at their local colleges. Those who do resits or start a GCSE course after Year 11 will be able to study the course in just one year.

AS levels (Advanced Supplementary Level)

Many sixth forms and schools offer this course which is equivalent to half an A level. They can either be studied as the first half of an A level or as a qualification in their own right. AS levels usually take one year of study to complete. If you take two AS levels with two A levels you could choose a broader range of subjects to study. AS level courses can be for one or two years and are accepted by most universities and polytechnics in addition to your A levels.

A levels (Advanced Level)

A levels are academic qualifications which provide a well-established and accepted route to degree courses and university. They are similar to AS levels but take two years to complete. Once you have passed the AS level in a subject you can opt to study the subject in more depth by taking the second half of the A-level course known as A2. The A2 is not a qualification in its own right.

You will usually need at least four Grade C GCSEs to be able to cope with A-level study. A levels usually take two years to complete and while most people take three subjects, some take two with other studies making up their timetable.

Highers and Advanced Highers

These are the Scottish equivalent of AS and A levels, taken in the last two years of school respectively. The difference is, your Higher grade does not count towards your Advanced Higher grade, so Sixth Year (Year 13) is a fresh start. Usually, entrance to university is based on Advanced Higher results, a pass being grades A-C. They are the same standard and worth the same number of UCAS points as A levels. For more information on qualifications available to Scottish students (Standard Grade, Higher or Advanced Higher) see this quick guide by the Scottish Qualifications Authority: http://www.sqa.org.uk/files_ccc/NQQuickGuide.pdf

General National Vocational Qualifications (GNVQs)

GNVQs are intended for young people aged 16 to 19 who are in full-time education. They offer you a vocational alternative to traditional academic qualifications. GNVQs provide a general education plus skills, knowledge and understanding, which will prepare you for work or further study. GNVQs are available at three levels:

1. Advanced – the advanced level is usually a two-year course, and is generally regarded to be equal to two A levels.
2. Intermediate – the intermediate level is usually a one-year course, and is generally regarded to be equal to four GCSE passes at grades A, B and C.
3. Foundation – the foundation level is equivalent to GCSEs at grades D to G.

National Vocational Qualification (NVQ)

NVQs are for anyone aged 16 and over. They offer recognised vocational qualifications which are valued by employers because they demonstrate that you have the high quality skills required at work. Don't confuse them with GNVQs, they are completely different. NVQs are available at five levels:

⇨ Level 1 – Foundation
⇨ Level 2 – Basic craft
⇨ Level 3 – Technician, advanced craft, supervisor
⇨ Level 4 – Higher technician, junior management
⇨ Level 5 – Professional, middle management.

The Learning and Skills Council

The Learning and Skills Council is responsible for funding and planning education and training for over-16-year-olds in England. Taking over from the Training and Education Councils (TECs), their mission is to raise participation and attainment through high-quality education and training which puts learners first.

⇨ The above information is reprinted with kind permission from TheSite.org. Visit www.thesite.org for more information.

© TheSite.org

England's National Curriculum evolves

Information from the Department for Education and Skills

When the National Curriculum for England was first introduced in 1988, its aim was to ensure a broad and balanced education for all pupils. It defined the depth and breadth of study for pupils across four phases of their school career:

⇨ Key Stage 1 (ages 5-7);
⇨ Key Stage 2 (7-11);
⇨ Key Stage 3 (11-14);
⇨ Key Stage 4 (14-16).

The curriculum has evolved, with the latest changes aimed at improving standards while easing the burden on teachers.

In its early years, the National Curriculum attracted considerable criticism. The most high-profile objection was to the new testing regime, but people also said that:

⇨ the curriculum itself was too inflexible;
⇨ the new compulsory content took up too much curriculum time and put extra pressure on the school day.

A revised curriculum, introduced in 1995, addressed some of these problems. It reduced the amount of compulsory content and abandoned compulsory testing outside the core subjects.

Since then, there have been many reforms focusing on raising standards in these core subjects. Pupils' attainment has improved, but there are concerns that this focus could reduce the breadth and depth of learning in the non-core subjects.

Recent reforms have sought to encourage improvement in the core subjects within a broad and rich curriculum.

A broad curriculum can help learning in core subjects

Ofsted's report on the curriculum in successful primary schools (2002) looked at 30 schools. They had all achieved high standards in the core subjects within a broad and rich curriculum.

It is widely accepted that experiencing a variety of academic and non-academic subjects is, in itself, an important part of education. Ofsted suggested that a broad curriculum could also help to raise standards in core subjects.

It is widely accepted that experiencing a variety of academic and non-academic subjects is, in itself, an important part of education

---

In particular, Ofsted felt that arts subjects helped to stimulate pupils' imaginations. They learned to use media and materials more creatively, and grew in self-confidence. This helped them to tackle challenging work, and promoted positive attitudes towards school.

Though most taught subjects within the curriculum separately, teachers in the successful schools would often make links between them. Ofsted suggested that these links could:

⇨ make the curriculum more coherent and relevant to pupils;
⇨ reinforce pupils' learning by allowing them to use skills developed in a different subject;
⇨ increase pupils' depth of understanding by allowing them to study a single theme across different subjects.

Balance in the current curriculum

Ofsted evaluated the impact of the Primary National Strategy in primary schools in 2005. It found that the school leaders were increasingly focused on raising standards in core subjects. But schools had been more cautious in adopting a more flexible approach to the curriculum.

The 14-19 Education and Skills White Paper (2005) argued that the current 14-19 curriculum leaves little time for schools to provide

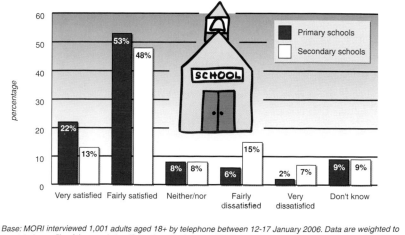

Satisfaction with schools

Respondents were asked: 'I am going to read out a list of public services. From what you know or have heard, please tell me how satisfied or dissatisfied you are with the way each service is provided for Britain as a whole?'

- Primary schools
- Secondary schools

Very satisfied: 22%, 13%
Fairly satisfied: 53%, 48%
Neither/nor: 8%, 8%
Fairly dissatisfied: 6%, 15%
Very dissatisfied: 2%, 7%
Don't know: 9%, 9%

Base: MORI interviewed 1,001 adults aged 18+ by telephone between 12-17 January 2006. Data are weighted to match the profile of the population. Taken from the Ipsos MORI 'Britain Today' survey. Source: Ipsos MORI 2006.

catch-up classes for those who have fallen behind. It also said there were not enough opportunities to stretch higher-attaining pupils.

Revised frameworks for primary schools

From September 2006, primary schools have had revised frameworks for teaching literacy and maths. They are designed to:
⇨ support further increases in standards;
⇨ reduce teacher workload and encourage more long-term planning.

The curriculum has evolved, with the latest changes aimed at improving standards while easing the burden on teachers

---

The new frameworks also emphasise the role of the wider curriculum in developing skills in literacy and maths. They encourage schools to take a more flexible approach, exploring opportunities to develop these core skills in other subject areas.

A shift in focus for secondary schools

In 2005 the Qualifications and Curriculum Authority (QCA) launched a review of the Key Stage 3 curriculum and elements of the curriculum at Key Stage 4. A national consultation runs from February to April 2007.

The changes at Key Stage 3 will mark a shift in focus:
⇨ less emphasis on setting out the content of lessons;
⇨ more on key concepts and skills.

This will make the curriculum more flexible, allowing schools to do more to personalise learning for individual pupils. It wll create more time for activities that stretch pupils, including the most able. It will also give some pupils, especially those falling behind in English and maths, extra opportunities to catch up.

The new curriculum will encourage pupils to explore themes across different subjects, and to make connections across different areas of learning, increasing the depth of their understanding.

The review will also introduce minor changes at Key Stage 4, to:
⇨ ensure a smooth transition between Key Stages 3 and 4;
⇨ allow students to take full advantage of new opportunities becoming available at ages 14-19.

The Government is also exploring the possible advantages of some schools offering a condensed Key Stage 3. A number of pilot schools have taught the Key Stage 3 curriculum over two years instead of the usual three. The free year has been used for a variety of purposes, such as:
⇨ providing a wider curriculum with enrichment activities in Year 9;
⇨ spending an extra year on GCSE courses;
⇨ allowing pupils to take some GCSEs early.

More flexibility and new subjects in 14-19 education

Reforms to 14-19 education will introduce a new, more flexible entitlement. As well as studying the core subjects at GCSE, students will have the opportunity to follow a range of specialised diploma courses in new subjects.

Consultation on raising individual achievement and progress

The Secretary of State for Education and Skills, Alan Johnson, launched a consultation on 8 January 2007, on a four-pronged approach to ensure an increased focus on pupils' individual progress in schools. The consultation, Making Good Progress, asks what more can be done to help schools, parents and pupils without compromising improved standards. It closes on 2 April and the Government will publish its response by the end of April 2007.

Where can I find out more?

DirectGov and ParentsCentre have further information about the current national curriculum for England.

DirectGov also has links to information about the national curriculums for Wales, Scotland and Northern Ireland.

⇨ The above information is reprinted with kind permission from the Department for Education and Skills. Please visit their website at www.dfes.gov.uk for more information.

© Crown copyright

PERSONALISED LEARNING·LESSON CONTENT·KEY CONCEPTS·SKILLS·CURRICULUM FLEXIBILITY·SPECIALISED DIPLOMA COURSES...

Today's learners and learning

What pupils think of the National Curriculum

By Pippa Lord

Do pupils think the curriculum is relevant? Do they enjoy it? Do they find it manageable? How do they want to learn and be assessed? What might teachers and policy-makers do?

The increasing focus on pupils' views in research and practice is clearly reflected in a review of pupils' views and experiences of the National Curriculum. *Pupils' experiences and perspectives of the National Curriculum and assessment*, commissioned by the Qualifications and Curriculum Authority and carried out by the NFER, is based on evidence amassed from over 300 sources published between 1989 and 2005. The review includes large-scale research projects and examples of smaller-scale, school-based action research.

What does this large body of evidence highlight for today's learners and learning? What pointers are there for teachers and policy-makers in the current contexts of assessment for learning, enjoying and achieving and personalised learning?

Some key findings

The review draws out the findings that have implications for current policy, as well as those that are raised by learners as much today as they have been throughout previous years.

'Passing exams'

⇨ Learners' views on the relevance of the curriculum are mainly associated with 'getting grades', but they also highlight the importance of real-life connections, and vocational and practical application.

'It's OK ... whatever'

⇨ Pupils' enjoyment of the curriculum seems to decrease across the key stages, including a dip in year 8 (a year with 'no focus', 'in limbo'). However, there is some improvement in pupils' enjoyment in key stage 4, particularly of optional subjects.

'Too much ...'

⇨ The right level of challenge is important to pupils' engagement, enjoyment, progression and achievement. They often say there is 'too much writing' and there are 'too many facts'. They recommend slimmer subject content, although not necessarily less depth.

Photo: Jean Scheijen

'Variety ... is the spice of life'

⇨ Pupils like variety. They want to learn through a variety of approaches, including teacher-supported and self-directed learning. Older pupils in particular like some individual responsibility and autonomy in their learning.

⇨ Pupils also like a variety of assessment methods (e.g. formal and informal, teacher-, self- and peer-led assessment, and ongoing and 'final' markers). They do like clear-cut grades, though, to gauge their progress.

⇨ Pupils like a variety of subjects to be on offer, including a balance between academic subjects and those that are more creative, practical or vocational. Within this variety, they want both personal choice and entitlement – particularly 'basics' for all, vocational learning for all, and careers guidance for all.

What might teachers and policy-makers do?

Pointers for teachers include making even more explicit the relevance and practical application of the curriculum for pupils, highlighting clear-cut markers and measures to help them gauge their progress, and providing opportunities for learners' personal choice and responsibility.

This might mean including a balance between ongoing assessment and 'final grades' around assessment for learning, even greater emphasis on practical application and personal choice to help pupils enjoy and achieve, and ensuring entitlement within a breadth and range of subjects, as well as personal choice – catering for pupils who like variety and pupils who prefer specialisation.

The final report for the review is available at: www.nfer.ac.uk/research-areas/pims-data/summaries/pupils-experiences-and-perspectives.cfm. For more information contact Pippa Lord, p.lord@nfer.ac.uk, telephone: 01904 433435.
24 November 2006

⇨ The above information is reprinted with kind permission from the National Foundation for Educational Research and the Qualifications and Curriculum Authority. Visit www. nfer.ac.uk or www.qca.org.uk for more information.

Education and ethnicity

Chinese pupils have best GCSE results

GCSE performance

In 2004 Chinese pupils were the most likely to achieve five or more GCSE grades A*-C in England, with 79 per cent of Chinese girls and 70 per cent of Chinese boys respectively. Indian pupils had the next highest achievement levels: 72 per cent of Indian girls and 62 per cent of Indian boys achieved these levels.

The groups most likely to have degrees were Chinese (31 per cent), Indian (25 per cent) and White Irish (24 per cent)

The lowest levels of GCSE attainment were among Black Caribbean pupils, particularly boys. Only 27 per cent of Black Caribbean boys and 44 per cent of Black Caribbean girls achieved five or more A*-C grade GCSEs. Pupils from the Black African, Other Black and Mixed White and Black Caribbean groups had the next lowest levels of attainment.

Within each ethnic group a higher proportion of girls than boys achieved five or more GCSE grades A*-C (or equivalent).

School exclusions

In 2003/04 pupils from Black Caribbean, Other Black and Mixed White and Black Caribbean groups were among the most likely to be permanently excluded from schools in England.

The permanent exclusion rates for pupils from the Other Black, Black Caribbean and Mixed White and Black Caribbean groups were 42 pupils per 10,000, 41 per 10,000 and 37 per 10,000 respectively. These were up to three times the rate for White pupils (14 pupils per 10,000). Chinese and Indian pupils had the lowest exclusion rates, at 2 or less pupils excluded per 10,000.

For all ethnic groups, the rate of permanent exclusions was higher for boys than girls, with boys representing around 80 per cent of the total number of permanent exclusions.

Highest qualification

In 2004 people from the Bangladeshi, Black Caribbean and Pakistani groups were less likely than White British people to have a degree (or equivalent).

Among men, Bangladeshis and Black Caribbeans were the least likely to have a degree (11 per cent for each group). Among women, Bangladeshis and Pakistanis were the least likely to have a degree, five and 10 per cent respectively.

The groups most likely to have degrees were Chinese (31 per cent), Indian (25 per cent) and White Irish (24 per cent). These compared with 17 per cent of White British people. However, a relatively high proportion of Chinese people had no qualifications – 20 per cent, compared with 15 per cent of White British people.

Bangladeshis and Pakistanis were the most likely to be unqualified. Five in ten (49 per cent) Bangladeshi women and four in ten (40 per cent) Bangladeshi men had no qualifications. Among Pakistanis, 35 per cent of women and 29 per cent of men had no qualifications.

Sources

Department for Education and Skills, National Curriculum Assessment, GCSE and Equivalent Attainment and Post-16 Attainment by Pupil Characteristics in England 2004, Statistical First Release 08/2005.

Pupil Level Annual Schools Census (PLASC) and Termly Exclusions Survey, Department for Education and Skills.

Annual Population Survey, January 2004 to December 2004, Office for National Statistics.
Published on 21 February 2006

⇨ The above information is reprinted with kind permission from the Office for National Statistics. Visit www.statistics.gov.uk for more information.

© Crown copyright

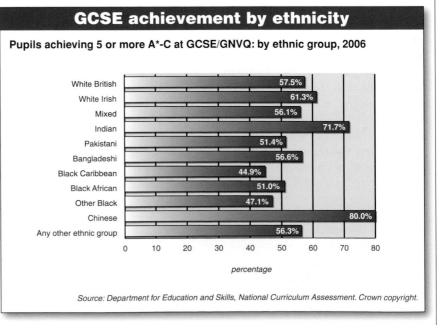

GCSE achievement by ethnicity

Pupils achieving 5 or more A*-C at GCSE/GNVQ: by ethnic group, 2006

Ethnic group	Percentage
White British	57.5%
White Irish	61.3%
Mixed	56.1%
Indian	71.7%
Pakistani	51.4%
Bangladeshi	56.6%
Black Caribbean	44.9%
Black African	51.0%
Other Black	47.1%
Chinese	80.0%
Any other ethnic group	56.3%

Source: Department for Education and Skills, National Curriculum Assessment. Crown copyright.

Report brands schools institutionally racist

A Government report that brands schools as 'institutionally racist' has caused anger amongst teachers

The report, *Getting It. Getting It Right*, leaked to the *Independent on Sunday*, reveals 'systemic racial discrimination' in the country's education system, with three times more black children being excluded than whites.

Furthermore, black children were also five times less likely to be officially registered as 'gifted and talented'. The bias was 'largely unwitting' due to the negative stereotype of black people as threatening, the report noted.

But education unions said there was no evidence that teachers were racist and insisted pupils were simply thrown out for being badly behaved.

The report was initially ordered by the Government to find out why so many black pupils were being thrown out of school. Every year 1,000 black pupils are permanently expelled from school and 30,000 more are banned for a limited period.

The accusation that schools are 'institutionally racist' could have damaging consequences because schools and other public bodies are required by law to eliminate unlawful racial discrimination.

The report, written by Peter Wanless, director of school performance and reform at the Department for Education and Skills, states: 'The exclusions gap is caused by largely unwitting, but systematic racial discrimination in the application of disciplinary and exclusions policies.'

The report concludes: 'A compelling case can be made for the existence of "institutional racism" in schools.

'Even with the best efforts to improve provision for excluded pupils, the continued existence of the exclusion gap means that black pupils are disproportionately denied mainstream education and the life chances that go with it.'

The report said there was a 'comparatively weak basis' for arguing that street culture had a more persuasive influence on black young people than it has on other young people. It blamed the portrayal of black 'street culture' for 'encouraging school staff to expect black pupils to be worse behaved and to perceive a greater level of threat'.

But teachers' leaders said there was no justification for the report's findings.

Mick Brookes, General Secretary of the National Association of Head-teachers, said: 'In my experience as a head teacher my colleagues have always shown absolute integrity in how all young people are treated.'

John Dunford, the general secretary of the Association of School and College Leaders, said: 'I think schools are very racially tolerant places in comparison with what can happen in society outside their gates.'

Philip Parkin, General Secretary of the Professional Association of Teachers, said: 'Schools cannot be regarded as the panacea for all of society's failings.

'There is no justification for branding the education system institutionally racist when only a very small percentage of schools may be giving cause for concern.'

Chris Keates, General Secretary of the NASUWT, said: 'We don't believe that schools want to address behaviour problems on the basis of race of the pupil. Our evidence simply doesn't show that.'

John Bangs, head of education at the National Union of Teachers, said the evidence that black boys were five times less likely to be identified as gifted and talented was more of a class issue, adding: 'You could apply this statistic just as easily to white, working-class boys.'

Shadow Education Secretary David Willetts said: 'We do need to tackle this problem, but labelling our schools "institutionally racist" doesn't help.

'We should be focussing on raising educational standards and tackling truancy – not throwing around allegations of racism.'

Former Conservative Minister Edwina Currie told Sky News: 'If it were a racist issue then it would be affecting young Asians. Young Chinese do extremely well.'

Three times more black children are being excluded than white

---

A spokesman for the Commission for Racial Equality said: 'We have long said that there are differential outcomes for different ethnic groups in terms of achievement, especially in the case of young black boys.

'However, the cultural outlook for this group is also a factor. The CRE believes black children need role models and, ideally, parents to play a more active role in their children's education.'

An Education Department spokesman said: 'In the light of this work, ministers concluded that it would be inaccurate and counterproductive to brand the school system as racist. However, there is more that schools, parents and the Government can do to ensure that every child fulfils their potential whatever their background.'
11 December 2006

⇨ The above information is reprinted with kind permission from Teaching Times. Visit www.teachingtimes.co.uk for more information.
© Teaching Times

Education and gender

Girls outperform boys

Girls generally perform better than boys at GCSE and at GCE A level (or equivalent) in the UK. In 2004/05, 62 per cent of girls in their last year of compulsory education achieved five or more GCSE grades A* to C, compared with 52 per cent of boys.

The difference in achievement between the sexes starts at an early age. In England, from Key Stage 1 (five to seven years old) through to Key Stage 4 (14 to 16 years old) girls scored consistently higher than boys, although the difference was less marked in mathematics and science than in English. For Key Stage 2 (seven to 11 years old) mathematics, boys performed as well as girls in teacher assessments in 2005 and slightly better in the test component.

Over recent years there has been an increase in the proportion of both young men and young women in the UK gaining two or more GCE A levels (or equivalent). This increase has been more marked among young women. Between 1990/91 and 2004/05 the proportion of young women gaining this result more than doubled from 20 per cent to 45 per cent. Over the same period, the proportion of young men gaining this result increased from 18 per cent to 35 per cent.

At A level (Highers in Scotland) young women outperformed young men in virtually all subject groups in the UK in 2003/04. With the exception of French and Spanish, a greater proportion of women than men achieved grades A to C. In Gaelic and English Literature, both sexes achieved approximately equal numbers of A to C grades.

In 2004/05 more women than men in the UK were awarded National Vocational Qualifications (NVQ) and Scottish Vocational Qualifications (SVQ) at all levels. This was most noticeable at level 3 where nearly two-thirds of NVQs/SVQs awarded were to women. Of over half a million NVQs/SVQs awarded, 56 per cent were made to women compared with 44 per cent to men.

There were differences in the subjects taken by men and women for vocational qualifications. Nearly all vocational qualifications awarded for construction, planning and the built environment were to men and a negligible amount to women. This compared with around 90 per cent of vocational qualifications for health, public services and care being awarded to women.

Among those who took first degrees at higher education institutions in the UK in 2004/05, men and women were almost equally likely to gain a first – 11 per cent and 10 per cent respectively. However, a greater proportion of women achieved an upper second – 46 per cent of women compared with 39 per cent of men.

Sources

Education and Training Statistics for the United Kingdom, 2004/05, Department for Education and Skills; National Assembly for Wales; Scottish Executive; Northern Ireland Department of Education; Higher Education Statistics Agency.

Notes

Data for pupils attaining five or more GCSE grades A* to C are as a percentage of all pupils in their last year of compulsory education. Data for 1992/93 to 1994/95 are for Great Britain.

Data for GCE A level achievement count two AS levels as one A level pass. Two A levels are equivalent to three or more Highers in Scotland. Pupils in Scotland generally sit Highers one year earlier than those sitting A levels in the rest of the UK. Data are for pupils in schools and further education institutions. Data prior to 1995/96, and for Wales and Northern Ireland from 2002/03, relate to schools only.

Published on 16 October 2006

⇨ Information from the Office for National Statistics. Visit www.statistics.gov.uk for more.

GCSE achievement by gender

Pupils achieving five or more GCSE grades A* to C or equivalent: by sex, UK

Girls

Boys

percentage

80
60
40
20
0

1995/96   2000/01   2002/03   2003/04   2004/05

TEST
F

Source: Education and Training Statistics for the United Kingdom, 2004/05, Department for Education and Skills; National Assembly for Wales; Scottish Executive; Northern Ireland Department for Education; Higher Education Statistics Agency. Crown copyright.

Gender and subject choice

Information from the Standards Site

⇨ While girls are now achieving better academic results than boys at age 16, relatively few young women are choosing science or science-related subjects for further study.

⇨ Boys dominate in maths, science and technology at A level and far more men than women study these subjects in higher education. This has significant implications for men's and women's career choices and future earnings: 60% of working women are clustered in only 10% of occupations; and men are also under-represented in a number of occupations.

⇨ Pupils' subject and course choices are influenced by a range of factors: their own views and expectations, those of their peers, parents and teachers, and the media.

Some words of warning:

⇨ Most single-sex girls' schools are in the Independent sector; this makes for difficult comparisons with a national picture, as it is likely that any differences are artefacts of the Independent/Maintained split rather than the gender difference.

⇨ Although the list of subjects on our website attempts to classify what are traditionally 'feminine' areas of the curriculum, in today's world, such stereotyping is difficult to pin down – is, for example, medicine a 'traditionally' masculine career choice? 30 years ago, this might have been true, but it could be argued that it is no longer the case.

⇨ There is a problem over deciding what is 'choice' in terms of a school system (i.e. the choices pupils make for subjects studied). At GCSE there is still some restriction (both in terms of curriculum requirement and what the school opts for en bloc or by being a Specialist School), and it could be argued that only in a post-16 environment is there a true measure of 'choice'.

⇨ The above information is re-printed with kind permission from the Standards Site. Visit www.standards.dfes.gov.uk for more.

© Crown copyright

Single-sex schooling

New research dispels myths surrounding single-sex schooling

A study of people now in their 40s has revealed that those who went to single-sex schools were more likely to study subjects not traditionally associated with their gender than those who went to co-educational schools. Girls from single-sex schools also went on to earn more than those from co-educational schools.

The research, by the Institute of Education's Centre for Longitudinal Studies, has followed almost 13,000 individuals born in 1958 throughout their lives and so can tell us about longer-term consequences of types of schools.

The researchers found that at age 16, girls in girls' schools were more likely to gain maths and science A-levels, and boys in boys' schools more liable to gain A-levels in English and modern languages than their peers in co-educational schools. Girls and boys in single-sex schools also had more confidence in their ability to do well in these subjects.

The pattern carried through to university, with women from girls' schools more likely than co-educated women to gain qualifications in subjects typically dominated by men and to go on to earn higher salaries in their jobs.

Researcher Dr Alice Sullivan explains: 'Single-sex schools seemed more likely to encourage students to pursue academic paths according to their talents rather than their gender, whereas more gender-stereotyped choices were made in co-educational schools. This suggests that co-educational schools need to examine the ways in which they have, probably unwittingly, enforced powerful gender stereotypes on both girls and boys.'

Researcher Professor Diana Leonard says: 'Although having been to a single-sex school is not

significantly linked to a gender-atypical occupation, girls from single-sex schools do get higher wages in later life. This could be because they are carrying out more technical or scientific roles even within female-dominated jobs, for example, becoming science teachers rather than French teachers, or because they have learned to be more self-confident in negotiating their wages and salaries.'

But single-sex education brought almost no advantage in terms of exam results. Girls from girls' schools did only slightly better in exams than their co-educational peers. Boys did no better at all (allowing for differences in ability and family background). While girls at girls' schools were slightly more likely than girls in mixed schools to gain five or more O-levels at grades A-C, this advantage did not carry through to further and higher education. There was no impact of single-sex schooling on maths test scores at age 16, nor did single-sex schooling make it more likely for pupils to gain any A-levels at all, to get a university degree by age 33, or to enter high-status occupations.

Single-sex education brought almost no advantage in terms of exam results

---

Dr Sullivan says: 'Our research emphatically does not support the suggestion that achievement is higher in single-sex schools.'

Other findings showed that boys in boys' schools were more likely to dislike school than boys in co-ed schools, but both sexes were less likely to truant in single-sex schools.

Single-sex schooling appeared to have no impact on the likelihood of marriage or childbearing, or on the quality of partnerships formed. Neither did it appear to affect the division of labour in the home, nor attitudes to women's work outside the home. However, men who had attended single-sex schools were more likely to be divorced by age 42.

This research was funded by the Economic and Social Research Council.
22 September 2006

⇨ The above information is reprinted with kind permission from the Institute of Education, University of London. Visit www.ioe.ac.uk for more information.
© Institute of Education, University of London

Teacher numbers

There are more teachers in schools in England than at any time since 1981. However, there have been concerns that despite this increase, class sizes are rising

Are there really more teachers?

Yes. The number of full-time equivalent teachers is now 435,400 – its highest level for 15 years. At the same time the number of overseas-trained teachers and instructors has fallen. Vacancies are down as well, with the number of empty teaching posts halving since 2001.

Aren't support staff making up the numbers?

The number of support staff is up by 25,500 since January 2004 and by over 130,000 since January 1997. Critics argue that they provide teaching on the cheap. However, they undertake a very different role. Essentially, they free up time for teachers to concentrate on the children, taking on tasks from admin to small group work.

But are class sizes still rising?

No. Overall, the average infant (five- to seven-year-olds) class has 25.6 pupils, the same as last year. Average secondary school classes are 21.5 pupils.

Also important is the pupil to teacher ratio, in other words, the number of pupils per teacher. This has fallen from 22.5 to 22 in primary schools and from 16.7 to 16.6 in secondary schools.

Infant classes (five- to seven-year-olds) are limited by law to 30 or fewer pupils, in order to ensure children get enough attention. However, there are occasions when permission is given for a class to increase for a short period – for example to admit a pupil who has moved into the area during the school year.

In the last year there has been a small increase in the number of infant classes admitting more than 30 pupils (1.7 per cent of all classes for this age group). However, the average size remains 25.6 pupils.

Who wants to be a teacher?

In the past, teacher training was not always seen as an attractive option, as graduates were put off by the thought of another year of debt. So all postgraduate trainees now get a £6,000 bursary.

There are also other incentives for graduates from subjects where there are shortages of teachers. From September this year, graduates in shortage subjects (maths, science, English, modern foreign languages, music, technology and ICT) will receive a higher training bursary of £9,000.

Maths and science graduates will also receive a 'Golden Hello' of £5,000 when they complete their induction at their new school. There are 'Golden Hello' payments of £2,500 for graduates in other shortage subjects.

Overall, the number of teacher trainees has just risen for the fifth year running.

Routes into teaching are now much more diverse with over 10 per cent of teachers now coming through new flexible or employment-based schemes.

Teachers' pay

Teachers are better paid now too. Since 1997, starting salaries for newly qualified teachers have risen from just £14,280 to £19,023 outside London and from £16,341 to £23,001 in inner London.

For experienced teachers, pay is up from £21,318 to at least £28,000, and, in some cases, to more than £32,000 (£38,000 in inner London).

⇨ Information from the Department for Education and Skills. Visit www. dfes.gov.uk for more information.
© Crown copyright

Education and social mobility

Education systems have little impact on social mobility

Current debate about the government's proposed education reforms may be based on a false premise. Recent research suggests that education policy by itself contributes little to the rate at which people move between social classes, according to a new study funded by the Economic and Social Research Council (ESRC).

Comprehensive schooling is neither less nor more effective at promoting social mobility than a selective system, says the research carried out by Dr Cristina Iannelli and Professor Lindsay Paterson of the University of Edinburgh.

Recent research suggests that education policy by itself contributes little to the rate at which people move between social classes

---

If changes to the structure of schooling could have an effect, then it should show in Scotland, where all selective schools in the public sector were abolished by the mid-1970s, they point out. Instead, they found that educational reforms had no impact either way.

While education may have provided the oil that lubricated upward mobility, the biggest effect has come through changes in the jobs people do, and how employment is structured.

The report says that though education has an intermediary role between where people start out and where they end up, its effect on social mobility has weakened. This suggests that middle-class parents must be finding other ways to give their children an advantage in life.

Analysing data from major sources including the Scottish Household Survey, the researchers also found that while there remains a great deal of movement in social status – mostly upwards – that trend is slowing.

Dr Iannelli said: 'Upward mobility has been common for at least five decades, and the parents of people born since the 1960s have themselves benefited from it to such an extent that there is less room for their children to move further up.

'At the same time, there is also little evidence of any increase in people slipping down the social ladder.'

By contrast, the report points to policies such as the Swedish kind of redistributive social democracy, or the social market of the type found in France and the Netherlands, as necessary for reducing inequalities of mobility.

They did, however, find some reduction in this inequality when people born in Scotland at the start of the 20th century were compared with those from after 1950.

The major difference between the sexes is that women are more likely to have lower non-manual jobs, while men tend to be in skilled-manual work. So women whose fathers were in manual employment are more likely to be in a non-manual job than men from similar backgrounds.

But Dr Iannelli said: 'We found also gender differences within industrial sectors. Women's main opportunity for upward mobility has been in services such as finance, health and education. However, women depend more on social background if they are to reach a professional position in something like banking or insurance.'

Looking to the future, the study sets out two possible scenarios. One is that if educational expansion continues, inequalities will start to fall significantly, particularly if jobs go to people on merit.

Alternatively, as middle-class families seek to prevent their children falling down the social ladder, there might be political pressure to distinguish between the value of educational results at the top end – for example, through some universities charging higher fees than others, a policy which the Scottish Parliament has resisted.

Dr Iannelli said: 'The best labour market rewards might then go to graduates from the highest status universities populated by the most middle-class students. In such circumstances, social inequality would at best remain unchanged, and could start to worsen for the first time in at least half a century.'

17 February 2006

⇨ The above information is reprinted with kind permission from the Economic and Social Research Council. Please visit their website at www.esrc.ac.uk for more information.

©ESRC

Academies

Information from the Department for Education and Skills

There are 27 Academies across the country, with more than 40 opening this year. The aim is to have 200 open by 2010. These new schools are helping raise standards in disadvantaged areas, but there are concerns over who is really profiting from Academies, and whether other local schools are losing out.

More pupils than ever are doing well at secondary level – with record GCSE and A level results recorded yet again last year. However, there are still too many schools, often in disadvantaged areas, where, despite the best efforts of heads, teachers and parents, the pattern of poor results and low aspirations has proved seemingly impossible to shift.

What are Academies?

Academies are independent state schools specifically charged with taking on this challenge. Some are brand new schools, others replace failing ones (those with 30 per cent or fewer students getting five GCSEs at A*-C).

They are set up as charitable companies by business, faith or voluntary groups and receive both sponsorship from that group and government funding. Their independent status allows them the flexibility to be creative in their management, governance, teaching and curriculum in order to meet local need.

They are all-ability schools, with a focus on one particular specialism, although they can have more. In line with other specialist schools, they can admit up to 10 per cent of their pupils on the basis of an aptitude for the specialism.

While they are not bound by the national curriculum, they must teach core subjects and carry out Key Stage 3 assessments in English, maths and science.

Where are they?

They were initially designated 'City Academies', but the Education Act 2002 allowed for their expansion into rural areas, and for the establishment of all-age, primary and sixth form Academies. They are set up in areas of deprivation, according to indices from the Office of the Deputy Prime Minister.

So far, 27 have opened, and many more are in development.

Are they fairly funded?

Questions have been raised as to whether Academies are getting the lion's share of government funding, at the expense of other local schools.

The government funds Academies' recurrent costs at a comparable rate with other maintained schools. They do get an initial substantial capital investment in their building – the sponsor provides around £2 million with the government meeting the balance – but this is simply sharing in the Building Schools for the Future programme, which is refurbishing or rebuilding every secondary over the next 15 years.

Around £5 billion will be spent on building the 200 Academies. Over the ten years to 2008, over £38 billion will be spent on other school buildings.

In addition, Academies share their facilities and expertise with other schools and the wider community, helping raise standards across the whole area.

Sponsors are bound by charity law to act in the best interests of the school and are subject to strict funding agreements. No one makes money out of Academies. The only people benefiting are the pupils and parents.

How are Academies performing?

There have been claims in the media that Academies, particularly those in London, are failing and that their GCSE results are languishing at the bottom of league tables.

GCSE results in Academies are improving year on year, with particularly strong performance in the third year since opening.

In 2003, their first year, an average 24 per cent of Academy pupils gained five or more good GCSEs (A*-C), compared to 16 per cent in their predecessor schools. In 2004, this rose to 28.7 per cent, and last year the improvement rate was three times the national average – 36 per cent of Academy pupils got five or more GCSEs at A*-C.

Academies are all-ability schools with a focus on one particular specialism, although they can have more

---

Greig City Academy in London reported a 27-point rise in the numbers gaining five or more good grades at GCSE – from 25 per cent in 2004 to 52 per cent in 2005.

These results do not put Academies at the top of league tables, but they show rapid and continued improvement. And, most importantly, Academies are popular, as evidence of oversubscription shows. An independent evaluation by PriceWaterhouseCoopers found that they are oversubscribed by an average 62 per cent. The survey also showed that Academies were the first choice for eight out of ten parents who responded.

Thamesmead Community College in Bexley had 111 year sevens in its final intake, while The Business Academy Bexley, which replaced it, had 550 first-choice applicants in its opening year.

⇨ The above information is reprinted with kind permission from the Department for Education and Skills. Visit www.dfes.gov.uk for more information.

© Crown copyright

The academies programme

Information from the National Audit Office

Most academies have made good progress in improving GCSE results, and the programme is on track to deliver good value for money. Performance is rising faster than in other types of schools although results in English and maths are low. Academies have cost more to build than other schools, but most academy buildings are high quality.

These are some of the main findings in today's NAO report to Parliament, which concludes that if the trends in raising attainment continue, the academies programme will meet its objective of raising attainment in deprived areas.

The full impact of the first academies will not be known for several years because all pupils who have taken GCSEs in academies have spent time in other secondary schools. Evidence so far indicates that performance is improving compared with the predecessor schools. Most academies' results remain well below the national average, but good progress is being made towards that target. Academies are raising the achievements of pupils from deprived backgrounds. Taking account of pupils' personal circumstances and prior attainment, academies are performing substantially better than other schools. Overall performance in English and maths is low, but the position improved with the 2006 GCSE results. Academies are also improving pupil attendance faster than other schools.

Most academies are not achieving good results at advanced level. This reflects in part a lack of priority given to sixth forms in academies' early years, the small size of most academy sixth forms and predecessor schools' historically low attainment. The report concludes that while there can be a good case for having a sixth form, the grounds need to be solid and address the potential risk of lowering the standards of post-16 education in the area.

One of the academies programme's three objectives is to drive up standards by raising achievement across the local area, but there has so far been little collaboration between academies and neighbouring schools. The Department expects new academies' first priorities to be improving education and standards, but as academies become better established themselves they need to step up collaboration so that their benefits are more widely spread in the communities in which they are located.

Two-thirds (17 out of 26) of the first academy buildings have suffered cost overruns averaging £3 million (the other nine were within their original budgets), and academies have cost an average of £24 million (£27 million for those that are entire new buildings) which makes them more expensive than other secondary schools. It is difficult to make direct comparisons with other new schools owing to differences in location, school size, site constraints and age range of pupils. Most academy buildings have been better designed and built, compared with a group of other new schools.

Today's report also states that the Department and HM Treasury need to agree on an appropriate way to enable academies to raise community usage above the 10 per cent threshold allowed under the regulations governing eligibility for VAT relief.

Sir John Bourn, head of the NAO, said today:

'Our report today shows that the academies programme is improving the standards of education and raising the achievements of pupils from deprived backgrounds. These are early days and more remains to be done, especially in improving English and maths results. The challenge for academies is to sustain the improvements while also spreading their benefits more widely in their communities.

'For the programme, the challenge is to manage capital costs better for the hundreds of new academies still planned to be built and to use the lessons from the programme, for example on good quality school buildings, to get good value for money for the large capital investment currently being made in academies and other secondary schools.'
23 February 2007

⇨ The above information is reprinted with kind permission from the National Audit Office. Visit www.nao.org.uk for more information.
© National Audit Office

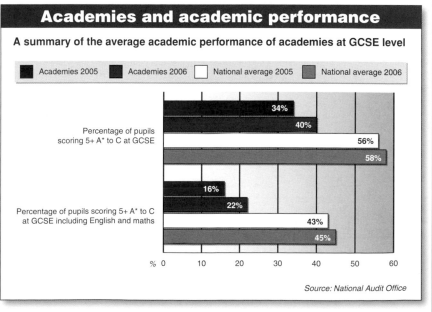

Academies and academic performance

A summary of the average academic performance of academies at GCSE level

- ■ Academies 2005
- ■ Academies 2006
- □ National average 2005
- ■ National average 2006

Percentage of pupils scoring 5+ A* to C at GCSE: 34%, 40%, 56%, 58%

Percentage of pupils scoring 5+ A* to C at GCSE including English and maths: 16%, 22%, 43%, 45%

% 0 10 20 30 40 50 60

Source: National Audit Office

Teacher opposition to academies grows

Information from the Sutton Trust

More than half of secondary school teachers in England and Wales (53%) do not think that setting up city academies is an appropriate way of raising standards in deprived areas, according to a MORI poll of secondary school teachers commissioned by the Sutton Trust and published today.

This is a significant increase from the 37% who said this in response to the identical question in last year's MORI poll commissioned by the Trust (which was set up in 1997 by Sir Peter Lampl, to help non-privileged children). Only 26% of teachers agreed with the Government's approach, down from 36% in 2004.

Furthermore, teachers express considerable doubt about the real impact of extending greater school choice to parents – another key element of the Government's White Paper. 60% of teachers do not think that school choice is a reality for most parents, compared to 29% who do, and 58% do not believe 'school choice' has improved standards, compared to 31% who do. Nearly half (48%) do not think the current system of admissions to secondary schools operates fairly, as opposed to 41% who think it does.

Barry Sheerman, MP, Chairman of the Education and Skills Select Committee, said: 'As a practical matter, school teachers have to implement the proposals contained in the White Paper and the Government should be concerned that the number of teachers who are against school choice and city academies, two key proposals, outnumber those in favour by a factor of 2:1.'

Sir Peter said: 'I think teachers have become more negative about academies because of their very high costs and concerns about sponsors who have little experience of managing educational establishments.'

More than half of secondary school teachers in England and Wales (53%) do not think that setting up city academies is an appropriate way of raising standards in deprived areas

---

More than eight out of ten secondary school teachers (82%) support changes which would enable students to apply to universities after they have received their A level results. Asked whether they supported the Government's proposal to introduce Post-Qualification Admission (PQA), rather than university offers being based, as now, on predicted grades, only 14% of the teachers surveyed thought it was a bad idea.

Sir Peter Lampl, Chairman of the Sutton Trust, said: 'This overwhelming support from teachers should encourage the Government to press ahead with the introduction of PQA which would be fairer for everyone – particularly able students in schools which traditionally send few students to the top universities. For these young people, often from less affluent backgrounds, having achieved exam success before they make their HE choices will give them the confidence to aim high and to apply to the country's leading universities.'

The MORI Teachers' Omnibus survey covered a representative sample of 477 secondary school teachers in maintained schools in England and Wales. It was carried out between November 4th and 24th, shortly after the White Paper, *Higher Standards, Better Schools for All* (which aims to bring about more choice for parents and pupils), was published on October 26th.

⇨ The above information is reprinted with kind permission from the Sutton Trust. Visit www.suttontrust.com for more information.

© Sutton Trust

Employers let down by schools

One in three employers is having to send staff for remedial training to teach them basic English and maths skills they did not learn at school, according to a new report by the Confederation of British Industry

Around a fifth of employers often find non-graduate recruits of all ages have literacy or numeracy problems, yet a third expect the levels of skills required for work will increase over the next five years.

The disturbing figures are contained in a CBI report commissioned by the Department for Education and Skills as part of its promise to raise basic skills levels through new functional skills modules for GCSEs.

It defines in detail what it means to be literate and numerate in the modern world of work – and also reveals what abilities in recruits employers would most like to see improved.

The opportunities for unskilled workers will shrivel from 3.4 million today to 600,000 by 2020

Simple mental arithmetic without a calculator, the ability to interpret data, competence in percentages, and calculating proportions top the numeracy wish list. Written communication including legible handwriting, communicating information orally, understanding written instructions, and correct grammar and spelling are the areas of literacy most in need of improvement.

Delivering these skills must be an integral part of our education system but, business says, it is not happening under the current GCSE curriculum.

Apart from the cost of having to pay for remedial training, UK businesses have to carry the burden in terms of low productivity, especially compared to their international competitors whose new recruits can boast higher functional skills.

Last year barely half of GCSE students achieved a Grade C or above in maths (54%) and just six out of ten (60%) in English. Only 45 per cent achieved both – the benchmark for competence in the three Rs. But the opportunities for unskilled workers will shrivel from 3.4 million today to 600,000 by 2020, according to Lord Leitch's interim report on skills in the UK.

CBI Director-General Richard Lambert said: 'We must raise our game on basic skills in this country. The UK simply can't match the low labour costs of China and India. We have to compete on the basis of quality, and that means improving our skills base, starting with the very basics.

'Employers' views on numeracy and literacy are crystal clear: people need to be able to read and write fluently and to carry out basic mental arithmetic. Far too many school-leavers struggle with these essential life skills.

'The fact that one in three employers ran remedial courses for their staff in the last year is a sad indictment of how the education system has let young people down. Acknowledging the problem and commissioning this report are first steps but the Government must show a far greater sense of urgency and purpose if it is to deliver on its promise to sort this out.'

Employers in the manufacturing and construction sector reported greater problems with innumeracy than in service industries. Both sectors reported a similar spread of literacy problems.

Businesses often find that employees who suffer from literacy and numeracy problems feel too ashamed to tell their manager. One personnel development manager at a business consultancy said: 'People become very adept at hiding their lack of literacy and numeracy. For instance one employee used to ask his wife to write his reports for him in the evenings.

'Another very capable employee hid his dyslexia very effectively but it came to light when he refused to apply for promotion. After two hours' discussion he finally said he could not write – the same individual now has a masters degree and is a champion for the "skills for you" training.'

The manager, who had previously been a head teacher at two secondary schools, added: 'A degree of creativity has been lost in secondary education, and with it the relevancy of learning that should prepare pupils for life. Schools should take into account the breadth of skills needed by school-leavers and make learning practical and relevant to their everyday situation.

'For example, pupils should be taught functional literacy and numeracy skills so that they can book a holiday, calculate 10 per cent off a sale item, or work out their pension contribution as a percentage of their salary.'

The problems are not confined to school-leavers and are washing through to the higher levels of the education system.

Figures from the CBI's Employment Trends Survey 2006 show nearly a quarter of employers (23%) were not satisfied with graduates' basic literacy and use of English, and 16 per cent had concerns about graduates' numeracy skills.

21 August 2006

⇨ Information from Teaching Times. Visit www.teachingtimes.co.uk for more information.

© *Teaching Times*

Success in mathematics fuels A-level achievement

Information from the Joint Council for Qualifications

The success of changes to the mathematics curriculum as a result of the review conducted by Professor Adrian Smith has contributed to this year's increase in achievement at A level.

The overall number of entries at A level in 2006 is at an all-time high at over 800,000 according to the entry and results data published today (Thursday 17 August 2006) by the umbrella group for the UK awarding bodies, the Joint Council for Qualifications (JCQ).

Girls now outperform boys at grade A in every major A-level subject, apart from modern foreign languages

---

There were 805,698 entries for A level this year, which is a 2.8 per cent increase on the figure of 783,878 entries for 2005.

The cumulative percentage of candidates attaining grades A-E increased by 0.4 per cent from 96.2 per cent to 96.6 per cent.

The overall results show an increase in the number of candidates achieving a grade A of 1.3 per cent (from 22.8 per cent in 2005 to 24.1 per cent in 2006) with the improvement at grade A in mathematics of 2.8 per cent (from 40.7 in 2005 to 43.5 in 2006) making a significant contribution to the total.

Increased take-up in mathematics is illustrated by an increase in entries for further mathematics of 22.5 per cent and mathematics of 5.8 per cent.

The overall figures show the performance of boys over girls at the pass grade has improved by 0.2 per cent compared with last year. However, at grade A the girls have moved further ahead by 0.2

per cent when compared with the performance of boys between 2005 and 2006.

Girls now outperform boys at grade A in every major A-level subject, apart from modern foreign languages.

The entry data for 2006 confirm traditional subjects such as biology, chemistry, English, geography, history and mathematics as the most popular.

There has been a significant increase in entries for chemistry (3.1 per cent) and biology (1.7 per cent). Physics saw a decrease in entries (2.7 per cent).

Entries to modern foreign languages are stable, with slight increases in French (1.1 per cent), German (5.1 per cent) and Spanish (4.7 per cent).

Commenting on the publication of the A-level entry and results data, Dr Ellie Johnson Searle, Director, Joint Council for Qualifications, said:

'The hard work of students and teachers is clear, especially when judged against the continuing rigour and robustness of the assessment system in the UK.

'The turnaround in mathematics – both in overall numbers and in achievement – is encouraging in the first year of the new specifications.'

AS level

There were 1,086,634 entries for all subjects at AS level in 2006, a 7,068 or 0.7 per cent increase (1,079,566 entries in 2005).

The top ten subject choices remain the same in 2006, with mathematics and further mathematics entries continuing to rise in 2006 with 3.9 per cent and 24.5 per cent increases respectively.

Despite the large fall in the number of GCSE entries in modern foreign languages in 2005, take-up of languages at AS level shows little overall knock-on effect, with Spanish entries rising (7.5 per cent),

no change in German (0.0 per cent) and French showing a slight decrease (2.8 per cent).

Results show an improvement overall, with a 0.5 per cent increase at grade A (to 18.4 per cent) and 0.2 per cent at grades A-E (to 87.5 per cent).

Applied AS

The new Applied AS Single and Double awards attracted 53,136 entries in their first year of operation (39,156 entries for Applied AS Single Award; 13,980 for Applied AS Double Award).

VCE (Vocational Certificate of Education)

The decline in entries for the VCE, phased out in 2006, testifies to the movement of candidates to the Applied GCE AS. For the VCE Advanced Subsidiary there was a decrease in entries from 19,849 to 3,093 (84.4 per cent), the VCE Advanced Single is down from 43,391 to 33,199 (23.5 per cent) and the VCE Advanced Double Award is down from 32,802 to 29,873 (9.0 per cent).

AEA (Advanced Extension Awards)

There were 11,099 entries for all subjects at AEA in 2006, a 1,794 (19.3 per cent) increase on 2005 (9,305 entries).

Achievements at distinction level fell by 0.1 per cent (from 17.2 per cent to 17.1 per cent) and at merit level by 1.2 per cent (from 49.4 per cent to 48.2 per cent) in 2006.

17 August 2006

⇨ The above information is reprinted with kind permission from the Joint Council for Qualifications. Visit www.jcq.org.uk for more information.

© Joint Council for Qualifications

Are exams getting easier?

Q. You think exams are too easy? A. You're stuck in the past. Education watchdog says claims of 'dumbing down' are out of date and elitist

Critics of Britain's exam system should stop trying to turn the clock back to the Fifties and accept that today's high-achieving students are the brightest generation of children the country has ever produced, according to the head of the government's exam watchdog.

Ken Boston, chief executive of the Qualifications and Curriculum Authority, confronted those who claim that rising pass rates are due to 'dumbed down' exams days before this year's A-level results for about 250,000 pupils in England and Wales emerge on Thursday.

He branded those attacking the system as 'elitists' who secretly hanker for the return of an era when only a tiny minority of secondary schoolchildren had the chance to go to university. Critics include Chris Woodhead, the former chief inspector of schools, the heads of some independent schools and the Institute of Directors. Woodhead last week alleged that educational 'prizes have become worthless', exam questions had been made less demanding and syllabuses had been dumbed down 'to the point where real intellectual challenge has disappeared'.

Boston said: 'The world has changed so much, yet many of the critics are still living in the Fifties, when only 10 per cent of youngsters continued in education beyond 17 and only four per cent went to university. My gut instinct is that those who take the position that standards have changed would really like to see us go back to the old system when only certain proportions of students could achieve a grade A, B, C or whatever, which meant that, say, only the top five per cent in any year could get an A grade and therefore go on to university. To have kept that system would have been absurd. These days 43 per cent go to university and secondary education is for everyone, not an elite.'

By Denis Campbell and Ned Temko

The Conservatives scrapped the system of pre-set limits on achievement, called 'norm referencing', in 1988 as part of a drive to encourage more pupils to stay on longer at school. Last year 96.2 per cent of the 783,878 A-level entries produced a pass, while 22.8 per cent resulted in an A.

Jim Knight, the Schools Minister, said A levels were just as tough as they had been for years

Jim Knight, the Schools Minister, said A levels were just as tough as they had been for years. 'More people are doing better at A levels every year since the system was changed in the Eighties, but that should not have been seen as lowering standards. Many more people doing well is a situation we should be celebrating.' He did not know if the relentless upward curve in passes and A grades would finally come to an end this week, although some experts privately believe that it might.

Critics are out of touch and do not appreciate how much education has changed to equip pupils for the modern world, added Boston. 'Maths students no longer calculate the square root of a large number manually, or learn how to use a slide rule, as I did in the late Fifties; they use calculators. Similarly the physics curriculum has developed so much over the last 15 years in response to the digital age that anyone of my generation who hasn't kept up with physics would find this year's A-level physics paper almost impossible.'

Educational innovation, better teaching and more students than ever before working harder to fulfil their potential explain the improvements in A-level results, not easier exams, according to Boston. 'The people who have trouble acknowledging that see education fundamentally as a device to sort the weak from the strong, and don't see that education is all about building the human capital of the nation and helping every individual reach their full potential – which we're better at doing than ever before. This annual circus of the "dumbing down" debate is a peculiarly English issue. It doesn't occur in other countries,' said Boston, an Australian.

But the QCA boss's broadside will not stop fresh claims of 'dumbing down' being made when the results are published on Thursday. Professor Alan Smithers, director of the Centre for Education and Employment Research at Buckingham University, said that, while A levels were in one sense harder for pupils because more young people are taking them, the exams themselves have been made easier.

Smithers highlighted the decision in 2000 to split two-year A-level courses into six parts, called 'modules', each of which is taken separately, as a key reason. 'Clearly if a course is broken into six bits, then it's a different task from having to show what you can do via highly pressured three-hour exams. That has made it easier to perform well, because it's easier to take one-sixth of the course than take the whole course at once, because there's less material to show you have a mastery of,' he said.

Students' right to retake individual modules in which they had done worse than expected, and freedom to drop subjects in which they perform poorly in the AS exams taken at the end of the lower sixth year, had both inevitably driven up the A-level pass rate. The increased stress on coursework, with pupils getting parental help or resorting to plagiarism using the internet, had also made it more straightforward to get good grades, said Smithers. 'To use an athletic analogy, when Roger Bannister ran the first four-minute mile in 1954 it was on a cinder track, but now running tracks are made of springy plastic and help runners turn in good performances. Similarly the conditions in which pupils do A levels have made it easier to get good results.' But an increased focus on exam results and school league tables has built-in incentives for schools and teachers to give pupils every help they can to achieve good grades, alleged the professor.

'Just as some athletes take performance-enhancing substances, so too a few schools and teachers succumb to the temptation of using performance-enhancing practices to help their pupils, for example by having a look at the exam paper in advance and then taking the students through the particular areas or even specific questions that are going to come up', said Smithers. 'While most do not use such tactics, most play to the limit of the rules, for instance by getting pupils to do coursework early, commenting on it, then getting the students to resubmit work which has been improved. That's legitimate, but doesn't distinguish between the performance of the children the way it should.'

The Confederation of British Industry and the Trades Union Congress also rejected claims of 'dumbing down'. 'We don't see the evidence of this, don't believe it's happening and don't think it's a big problem. The grade inflation debate distracts us from students' achievements,' said the CBI. Frances O'Grady, the TUC deputy general secretary, added: 'This is a critical time in young people's lives where they should be encouraged and supported.'

John Guy, the principal of 2,600-pupil Farnborough Sixth Form College in Hampshire, said more students are getting better A levels partly because the introduction of AS levels in 2000 has prompted more pupils to work harder during their two sixth-form years.

'Too many people are getting the highest possible grade. If I were a government minister now I wouldn't devise a system where 23 per cent get the top mark. An A-star would set a new challenge for talented youngsters,' he said.

Knight said that an A-star system may be introduced, depending on the outcome of pilot projects which the QCA is starting this autumn.

'I deserved my grades. I worked hard for them'

Myfanwy Liles and Luke Marriott exemplify the rising number of pupils getting A grades at A level. They both got As in maths, physics and computing at Weston College, Weston-super-Mare, Somerset, last August, while Luke also got a B in accounts.

Myfanwy, 19, studies physics at Liverpool University:

'The letter from Liverpool University saying they'd accepted me arrived on the day I was getting my results, so I already knew I'd got at least an A, a B and a C – their offer to me. But it was still really satisfying to open the envelope and see that it was three As. I felt I deserved my grades because I worked really hard for them, but so did a lot of my friends and they ended up with Cs or Ds.

'I have some sympathy with people who say exams are getting easier. For example, my maths course went from being three modules to four. That made it easier for me to get an A because there was less information to learn in each section.

'I suspect that over time exams are getting easier, partly because people are coming in off the back of doing GCSEs and haven't learnt things that they should know by 16 because GCSEs aren't as comprehensive as they could be.'

Luke, 19, studies computer science at Bristol University:

'When I got my results and saw it was three As and a B, I felt satisfied, fulfilled and proud, like I had achieved an accomplishment.'
13 August 2006

Emphasis on A-grades could lead to scientific skills gap

Siemens research shows pupils shun sciences for easier A-level subjects

New research published today by Siemens shows that many students who would like to take science, design technology and maths at A level are deterred by the emphasis on A grades for university entry.

Whilst the vast majority (over 80%) believe that science qualifications lead to interesting and well-paid jobs, the ability to get a high grade was a very important or important factor in deciding whether or not to make science or maths an A-level choice. The research comes at a time when there is increasing concern about growing shortages of the scientists, mathematicians and engineers needed for the UK's future prosperity.

70% of students believe that it is harder to get an A grade at A level in science-based subjects compared to 'softer' subjects

---

The major survey of 500 UK students, to investigate pupils' reasons for choosing their career-defining A-level options, reveals that 70% of students believe that it is harder to get an A grade at A level in science-based subjects compared to 'softer' subjects. When deciding whether or not to take a science subject, the level of difficulty in getting high grades is an important factor for 65% of students. Furthermore 66% factor in the balance between coursework and exams and 46% of pupils believe that the coursework accompanying science-based A levels is harder than that associated with other subjects.

How much they liked the subject teachers was an important factor for

74% of students and predictably, for 95%, how much they had enjoyed the subject at GCSE level.

The results come as the UK is currently suffering Europe's worst brain drain and will fall behind the rest of the world in science and research if this continues. Demand for science courses is falling (30% of university physics departments have merged or closed since 2001), whilst demand for science graduates is rising.

Alan Wood, chief executive of Siemens plc, said: 'The growing shortage of scientists, engineers and science and maths teachers will have serious long-term consequences for the UK unless we get more young people to take the subjects at least to A level.

'We feel it is time to consider innovations in how the subject is taught at GCSE level, the degree of support given during A levels and perhaps even a different points system for science and maths subjects. This is not to suggest "dumbing down"

the subjects at all, but we do need to ensure that students do not feel that if they choose harder subjects they will be less likely to get a place at a good university.

'Siemens is committed to generating interest in science amongst the next generation. We are currently sponsoring the "Building to the Limits" exhibition at the Science Museum and organising roadshows in schools throughout the country to show just how interesting the sciences can be. However, the situation needs to be addressed by a combination of government, schools, universities and employers if we are going to produce the highly-trained individuals that industry needs.'

The survey results have also attracted comment from the National Association of Head Teachers. Eric Frisk, Chairman, National Association of Head Teachers Secondary Committee, said: 'A-level results are at an all-time high and competition for university placements is extremely competitive.

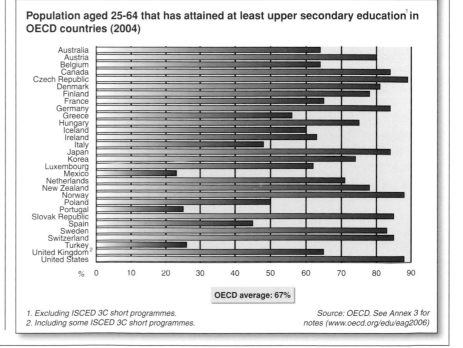

Upper secondary attainment

Population aged 25-64 that has attained at least upper secondary education[1] in OECD countries (2004)

OECD average: 67%

1. Excluding ISCED 3C short programmes.
2. Including some ISCED 3C short programmes.

Source: OECD. See Annex 3 for notes (www.oecd.org/edu/eag2006)

Consequently, students are taking "the safe" option when picking A levels at the expense of subjects like physics and chemistry that could potentially be more rewarding to themselves and of greater value to the economy.'

The UK is already in the unenviable position where only a quarter of schools have a physics teacher with a relevant degree* – a situation highlighted by the Royal Society, which too has called for urgent government action.

According to Jonathan Kestenbaum, CEO of the National Endowment for Science, Technology and the Arts (NESTA): 'Our recent "Real Science" research showed that there's a need to make science more engaging in the classroom through practical experiments. It makes science compelling for young people.

'We have to increase the take-up of science as the UK's global competitiveness will be founded on our capacity to meet ever greater demands for innovation.'

This research is part of Siemens Generation21 initiative, a worldwide Siemens programme to promote the education and training of young people. This is just one of the ways in which Siemens is honouring its commitment to society and fostering the innovators, leaders and creative talents of tomorrow.

As part of the same Siemens Generation21 initiative, Siemens and the Science Museum's Outreach Team, supported by a grant from Arts and Business, have been running science shows for schoolchildren in locations around the country, from Poole to Newcastle-upon-Tyne.

The shows take place in schools with which Siemens has local links and the subject matter relates to the 'Materials' module of the National Curriculum. They are highly interactive, entertaining and fun as well as educational. More shows are planned and will conclude in March with a visit to Nottingham, by which time more than 2,400 schoolchildren will have had the chance to experience a science show.

(* *Research statistics from the University of Buckingham, published 21 November 2005.*)
9 February 2006

⇨ The above information is reprinted with kind permission from Siemens. Visit the Siemens website at www.siemens.co.uk for more information.

© *Siemens*

57% 'did better than expected' in their exams

Information from Edexcel Limited

As the countdown to A-level results day begins, new research reveals that over half of UK adults actually did better than expected when they sat their exams. A survey commissioned by Edexcel has found that, when questioned about their past exam experiences, 57% of UK adults received better results than they were expecting.*

Jerry Jarvis, Edexcel's Managing Director, said: 'It is natural for students to be anxious about their exam results, it can be a stressful time, but the best advice we can give them is not to panic. Whatever the outcome of their results, there are always plenty of options available whether they want to continue in education or move in to the world of work.'

Edexcel's student-dedicated website, www.examzone.co.uk, is a one-stop shop for advice and guidance on all aspects of exam results, including an explanation of examination slips and information about resits and remarks.

Examzone also features:
⇨ free tips and timetable help for students
⇨ easy access to a bank of almost 2,000 past papers at an affordable price for both students and teachers
⇨ a growing number of model answers with examiners' explanations and mark schemes to aid students and teachers
⇨ free downloadable 'last-minute learner sheets' and clear glossaries from the Bitesize Revision guides for students.

* *The Exam Results Survey commissioned by Edexcel, was carried out by Tickbox.net between 25 July 2006 and 2 August 2006 and achieved a total sample of 1,766 UK adult responses, from which 1,581 respondents had already taken GCSEs or O levels.*
14 August 2006

⇨ The above information is reprinted with kind permission from Edexcel Limited. Visit www.edexcel.org.uk for more information.

© *Edexcel Limited*

Countdown to specialist diplomas

New qualifications will be available to all by 2013, the government says

By Peter Kingston

Within seven years, all other things being equal, the country will have a new education system with a new unit of currency. Labour says that by 2013 the 'specialist diploma' will be available to every young person aged between 14 and 19 who wants to study for one. There will be 14 varieties, or 'lines of learning', which can be studied at three levels.

> **Labour says that by 2013 the 'specialist diploma' will be available to every young person aged between 14 and 19 who wants to study for one**

Each is linked to an employment sector, for instance retail, engineering, health and social care etc., but these are not – the government stresses – vocational qualifications. They are not being designed to funnel those who do them into particular occupations. They make youngsters 'work ready', not 'job ready'.

A seven-year lead time might look like a leisurely amble, given the rapidity with which Labour has churned out and junked some education policies since 1997.

In reality, the pace is hectic and it has to be. There is an immense amount to do. For a start, the specialist diplomas have to be created. Details of the first five are due to be released later this month.

Then comes the big selling job: to young people, their parents, colleges, schools, universities, employers and, not least, the awarding bodies.

All parties must buy into the diplomas for their success. Two of them – schools and colleges – are receptive.

What about old qualifications?

But, as was made clear when sixth-form college principals met for their summer conference in Cambridge, there are serious anxieties about some of the conditions attached to the new diplomas.

What is going to happen, for instance, to the current cluster of qualifications?

The government has said loud and clear that A levels and GCSEs are staying as the 'cornerstone' of the new system. They can be components of the new 'overarching' qualifications or pursued separately.

But what of the vocational qualifications that are such staple features of FE colleges? In particular, what about the BTEC national diplomas that have proved their popularity and resilience in fighting previous attempts to kill them off, notably the introduction of GNVQs (General National Vocational Qualifications) in 1992?

The official line is that there is no intention to kill off BTECs.

The new diplomas 'are not vocational qualifications', says Teresa Bergin, the officer at the Qualifications and Curriculum Authority (QCA) responsible for managing their development, setting standards and assuring their quality.

'They are a mixture of general and applied learning,' she says. 'There are important vocational qualifications out there. The last thing we would want is for them to disappear overnight because they are serving important functions now.'

The preferred solution would be to have BTECs and others – or parts of them – subsumed into the new system. 'If diplomas are to be the qualification of choice then clearly some of these qualifications will change to become the components of the diplomas.'

The first five specialist diplomas – construction and the built environment, creative and media, engineering, health and social care, and ICT – are to be piloted in selected areas from September 2008.

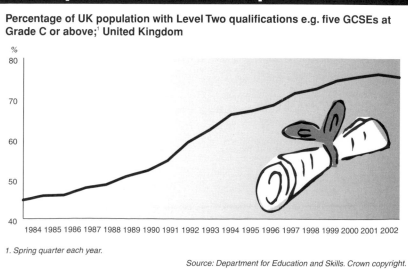

Population with Level 2 qualifications

Percentage of UK population with Level Two qualifications e.g. five GCSEs at Grade C or above;[1] United Kingdom

1984 1985 1986 1987 1988 1989 1990 1991 1992 1993 1994 1995 1996 1997 1998 1999 2000 2001 2002

1. Spring quarter each year.

Source: Department for Education and Skills. Crown copyright.

The unstated hope among politicians and officials must be that by 2013 these have made enough impact to wean colleges and young people off BTECs. If these linger, and significant numbers of schools and perhaps some sixth-form colleges plump to offer nothing but GCSEs and A levels, the new diplomas will find it much harder to get firmly established.

The level 1 version of a diploma will be done in one or two years, depending on the student, and will be for those 14-year-olds who are not ready to go into a level 2 diploma. This will be started in year 10 by the age group that typically begins preparing for GCSEs and will be completed in one or two years, depending on whether a student does other courses, for instance additional GCSEs.

The level 3 diploma will be achievable in two years of full-time study and will require the teaching time of a current three-A-level programme.

At each level the programme of study will come in three batches: generic, principal and additional learning.

'Generic' includes the functional skills of English, maths and ICT, learning and thinking skills and teamworking, as well as completion of a project. 'Principal' includes the study related to the employment sector in question, and 'additional' adds more of the same as well as other units that complement the sector.

The principal component in the level 1 construction and built environment diploma, for instance, will cover the design and creation of buildings, how they are valued and used and how they can be made sustainable.

The expectation is that no one school or college will be able to offer all 14 diplomas at three levels, or anything like. This is one reason why individual institutions are not able to apply to take part in the September 2008 pilot but had to apply in partnerships by the end of June. Presumably another reason is that a herd instinct will apply – colleges and schools that might otherwise have hung back will feel impelled to join the rush.

The government hopes also that

in their partnerships institutions will work out among themselves which of them will offer which bits of each diploma.

How successfully will erstwhile competitors be able to do this? In partnerships that have already begun the process the signs are very hopeful, says Bergin.

It is anticipated that students will have to move around between schools and colleges to complete their diplomas to a much greater extent than happens now.

This throws up a number of serious concerns, not just in rural areas where the journeys are likely to be considerable. Leaving aside any safety worries that parents might have, the obvious question is: who is going to pay? This has not been decided, but given the concerns in the sector about the lack of a national transport scheme for the present system, there is an immense amount of work to be done.

Students between colleges

One principal who has been involved in national discussions about the diplomas says: 'Schools will be concerned about their social control over young people who are no longer

with them all the time. And where will accountability lie for a student's performance?'

Which institution will take credit for the success of a young person who is flitting between two or even three?

The government, backed by the QCA, is insisting that every diploma at every level require the student to do at least 10 days' work experience. 'We are not talking about photocopying or making the tea,' says Bergin. This sounded an impossible and costly aspiration to the sixth-form college principals.

Greenhead College, Huddersfield, for instance, is held up as a leader in the effort and resources it puts into getting its students high-quality 'work shadowing'.

Even working at full tilt it is not possible to get placements for more than two-thirds, says Greenhead's principal, Martin Rostron, and this costs up to £50,000 a year. There simply may not be enough employers to accommodate the national student cohort. 'For 600 young people there are not enough employers in Huddersfield. We have to go much further afield, even to London.'

Who will own the diplomas? The QCA has begun negotiation with the big three awarding bodies and City & Guilds. If they are to lose business on their present batches of qualifications, no doubt they will each expect to be able to develop their own brands of some or all of the diplomas.

Employers obviously have to buy in to the new diplomas, which is the main reason why they have been offered a leading role in devising them.

Universities, too, have been brought in to the process. How higher education responds to diplomas will be critical to their success.

There is a lot of interest from universities, and not just from the former polytechnics, says Bergin.

But for the government the real breakthrough will only come when, for instance, a prestigious university accepts an applicant with a health and social care diploma to read medicine.

4 July 2006

© *Guardian Newspapers Limited 2007*

The specialised Diploma

A new 14-19 qualification will be available from September 2008

What is the Diploma?

QCA, the DfES and the Skills for Business Network are working together to develop the Diploma, which is a new qualification to recognise achievement at ages 14 to 19. It will combine practical skill development with theoretical and technical understanding and knowledge.

What is it for?

The Diploma will:
⇨ open up choices for young people
⇨ offer different ways of learning and a route into higher education or employment
⇨ provide credible, industry-verified applied learning, linked to interdependent general learning, with real opportunities to practise skills.

How will the Diploma be structured?

The Diploma will have three components:
⇨ principal learning – students develop knowledge, understanding, skills and attitudes relevant to a sector (or sectors) and are given opportunities to apply these to work roles or situations and realistic contexts
⇨ additional/specialist learning – students choose from a range of options endorsed by employers
⇨ generic learning – students develop and apply the skills and knowledge necessary for learning, employment and personal development.

The Diploma will be available at levels 1, 2 and 3:
⇨ level 1 Diploma will be comparable, in terms of average length of study, to a programme of four to five GCSEs
⇨ level 2 Diploma will be comparable, in terms of average length of study, to a programme of five to six GCSEs
⇨ level 3 Diploma will be comparable, in terms of average length of study, to a programme of three GCE A levels. A level 3 award is also being developed, broadly comparable in size to two A levels.

Diplomas may contain other qualifications or units.

The Diploma and the national curriculum

At key stage 4, learners follow the programme of study for the core and foundation subjects (English, mathematics and science, and ICT, PE and citizenship). One or more of these may fall inside a Diploma, depending on the scope and nature of the Diploma.

The Diploma and work experience

The Diploma will include a minimum of ten days' work experience at each level. A Diploma is different from an Apprenticeship. There will be clear routes between the specialised Diplomas and Apprenticeships. Specialised Diplomas may share units with an Apprenticeship.

What work has been done so far?

The structure of the Diploma has been developed by QCA and agreed by the Secretary of State. Diploma Development Partnerships (representing employers, higher education and other groups) have developed the content of Diplomas. Awarding bodies, working with the partnerships, are creating the qualifications from the agreed content.

There will be Diplomas for each of the 14 lines of learning as defined in the 14-19 White Paper. The development will be done in three stages.

By 2013 there will be a national entitlement for 14- to 19-year-olds to study towards any one of the specialised Diplomas.

Work on the specialised Diploma is part of a wider programme of 14-19 reform, taking forward proposals from the 14-19 Education and Skills White Paper.
September 2006

⇨ The above information is reprinted with kind permission from the Qualifications and Curriculum Authority. Please visit their website at www.qca.org.uk for more information.

© Qualifications and Curriculum Authority

The specialised Diploma

Subjects offered under the specialised Diploma

Lines of learning	Development
Information and communication technology	
Health and social care	
Engineering	First teaching: September 2008
Creative and media	
Construction and built environment	
Land-based and environmental	
Manufacturing	
Hair and beauty	First teaching: September 2009
Business administration and finance	
Hospitality and catering	
Public services	
Sport and leisure	
Retail	First teaching: September 2010
Travel and tourism	

Source: Qualifications and Curriculum Authority, September 2006.

Teenagers 'must stay in education till 18'

By Liz Lightfoot, Education Editor

Teenagers should be forced by law to stay in school or training up to the age of 18, the review of skills ordered by Gordon Brown said yesterday.

More than one in six young people leave school unable to read, write and add up properly and the proportion of 16-year-olds staying on in full-time education in the UK is below the average for developed countries, it said.

The proportion of 16-year-olds staying on in full time education in the UK is below the average for developed countries

---

The report by Lord Leitch, the chairman of Bupa and former chairman of Zurich Financial Services, warned the Government that its new vocational diplomas for 14- to 19-year-olds must succeed.

The first four of 14 new specialised diplomas will be introduced in 2008 covering ICT, engineering, health and social care and creative and media.

GCSEs and A levels will be incorporated into the new diploma framework, which will have a basic skills element.

'Once the Government is on track to successfully deliver diplomas,

demonstrated by rising participation at age 17, it should implement a change in the law, so that all young people must remain in full- or part-time education or workplace training up to the age of 18,' it said.

Teenagers are allowed to leave school after sitting their GCSEs in the academic year in which they turn 16 and only six in 10 are still in education and training by the age of 18. Last month Alan Johnson, the Education Secretary, signalled his support for a raising of the leaving age, saying that the policy had dramatically reduced the drop-out rate in Ontario.

The Canadians had decided that just as it was seen years ago as unacceptable to see a 14-year-old in work, so it should now be just as unacceptable to find a 16-year-old working without any education or training.

The 142-page report is the result of Lord Leitch's independent review to consider the skills base that the UK should aim to achieve in 2020 to maximise growth, productivity and social justice.

It points out that low levels of literacy, numeracy and technical skills are more likely to be a problem in recruits than existing employees.

Lord Leitch tells the Government that it needs to put employers firmly

in the driving seat of vocational qualifications and recommends a different way of funding training whereby further education colleges would not receive blocks of money but be forced to compete in the market place with private providers.

'In this country we have more than 22,000 vocational qualifications and we know that many of those deliver no value whatsoever,' he said.

The employer-led skills councils should decide what qualifications were appropriate for public funding.

The review said: 'Ensuring that only those qualifications approved by employers attract public funding will lead to a simplified qualification system, with fewer qualifications overall and only qualifications delivering economically valuable skills, attracting a return in the labour market, receiving public funding.'

The Chief Inspector of Schools said yesterday that it was a 'national disaster' that so many 11-year-olds were leaving primary school with poor reading skills.

Christine Gilbert, head of Ofsted, said standards were better than ever but needed further improvements.

Results of this year's national English tests showed 17 per cent of 11-year-olds were still failing to reach the expected standard in reading, one per cent worse than the year before.

7 December 2006

Home learning in the UK

Information from the Economic and Social Research Council

This article provides a brief overview of key information and statistics related to home learning. It is designed to provide a concise and informative introduction to a specific area of ESRC research.

The Open University, which teaches by distance learning, is the UK's largest university

Other fact sheets in this series on *The Digital Economy* and *Education in the UK* may also be of interest.

Defining home learning

Several different types of modern learning take place away from a traditional taught classroom environment and involve greater or lesser degrees of home learning. Some of these may also involve workplace or 'on the job' learning. 'Distance learning' or 'correspondence courses' involve study from home supported by sent course materials and tutorial support over the phone or Internet.

Open learning and flexible learn-

ing courses normally involve pre-arranged attendance at an institution according to the requirements and availability of the learner, and may involve a degree of home study.

Some parents opt to teach their children at home themselves rather than send them to a school and those children who do attend school usually complete homework.

Home schooling

Teaching children of school age (5-16) at home is referred to as 'home schooling' or 'home education'. Home-schooled children do not need to follow the National Curriculum nor do their teachers need to be qualified. Parents opting for home schooling cite a variety of reasons for teaching their children at home including bullying, dissatisfaction with mainstream school, a child's special educational need, religious conviction or simply lifestyle choice.

It is difficult to estimate precisely how many children are home schooled in the UK. In England and Wales, children who are home schooled from age five will never appear in pupil statistics. In Scotland statistics are kept and rapid growth has been noted, with a 39 per cent increase in home schooling in 2005/6. More anecdotal sources suggest there is growing interest in home education and home school co-operatives where parents come together to provide home schooling.

It is also difficult to establish whether home-taught children outperform school-taught children academically. Most of the research has been conducted in the USA, where home-taught children did perform better, but it is not clear that home education is the cause of these differences – for instance those home schooling their children may themselves be more academically able than average.

Rationale for home-based learning

Home-based learning and flexible study courses are increasingly incorporated into educational institutions' provision. Unlike formal, classroom-based learning, flexible study courses are designed to allow individuals to work and learn at a time, place and speed that suit their specific needs.

The Government encourages out-of-school learning. The (then) Schools Minister Jacqui Smith stated in 2005 that 'the Government considers that learning at home is an essential part of the good education to which all our children are entitled. (...A) well-organised homework programme helps children and young people to develop the skills and attitudes they will need for successful, independent lifelong learning.'

Homework

Government guidelines for amount of homework to be set for school pupils

School type	School years	Age	Amount of homework
Primary	years 1 and 2	5-7	1 hour per week
	years 3 and 4	7-9	1.5 hours per week
	years 5 and 6	9-11	30 minutes per day
Secondary	years 7 and 8	11-13	45 to 90 minutes per day
	year 9	13-14	1 to 2 hours per day
	years 10 and 11	14-16	1.5 to 2.5 hours per day

Source: Parents' Centre: Homework (2006) Department for Education and Skills (Accessed 18 January 2007). Taken from the ESRC factsheet 'Home Learning in the UK'.

Flexible and distance-learning arrangements are often important for parents of young children, carers, mobility-impaired people, older people, workers with busy schedules and young people with few qualifications.

Home learning is also essential where would-be students are not located near a college or institution, where the desired course is not taught locally, or where individuals may be studying overseas for a UK qualification.

The prevalence of home learning

The Open University, which teaches by distance learning, is the largest university in the UK. In 2004/5 it had over 173,000 students making it three times the size of the next largest UK university. The OU offers qualifications from certificate through to doctorate level and has Europe's largest MBA programme. It offers a mix of paper and online learning resources backed up with remote or face-to-face contact with a tutor. The OU discontinued its course broadcasts via TV and radio in 2006. Access to a PC is now an entry requirement.

Attempts to establish an 'e-university' in the UK, offering courses entirely online, proved less successful. Launched in 2000 by the Secretary of State for Education, it was expected to attract 250,000 students in its tenth year of operation, with gross profits of £110 million. However, the initiative attracted only 900 students at a cost of £50 million. Many other such online initiatives have foundered, largely in the wake of the burst of the 'dot-com' bubble.

Reliably estimating the average hours spent on homework by pupils of different ages is very difficult and there are few sources of data. The government publishes guidelines for the amount of homework children in England and Wales should be expected to complete. A survey of 2,000 parents reported by the BBC found two-thirds were concerned about there being too much homework.

'Learndirect' is an agency which provides opportunities via a network of over 2,000 online learning centres

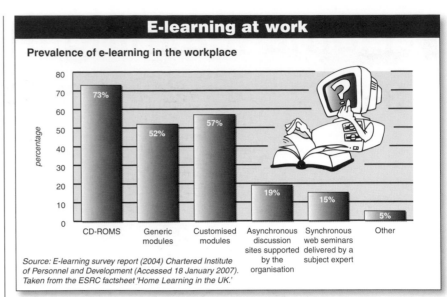

E-learning at work

Prevalence of e-learning in the workplace

Source: E-learning survey report (2004) Chartered Institute of Personnel and Development (Accessed 18 January 2007). Taken from the ESRC factsheet 'Home Learning in the UK.'

in the UK (excluding Scotland) for over-16s, concentrating particularly on those with few qualifications who are seeking skills for employment. Learndirect offers more than 550 courses which have enrolled around 1.3 million adults since 2000.

Research conducted at the University of London's Institute of Education and funded by the ESRC found 27 per cent of pupils were taught by private tutors outside of school, generally in mathematics and English. Although parents were generally satisfied with this form of home learning, there was only a small noticeable improvement in GCSE results.

E-learning and technological support for learning

The use of technologies such as the Internet, CD-ROMs and audio/video tapes to support personal study and education, has been termed 'e-learning'. This is a relatively new and rapidly evolving approach to learning, which can be used to support a range of different activities, including: distance learning, web-based learning and virtual classrooms.

The Chartered Institute for Personnel and Development noted that, within UK training provision, e-learning has seen one of the largest increases with a 47 per cent increase over the last few years, as compared to other learning opportunities such as external conferences and workshops (11 per cent) and formal classroom-based training (eight per cent). 26 per cent of workers believe that e-learning has significantly altered

their learning and training offerings but only one per cent think that e-learning is the most effective way to learn.

CD-ROM-based forms of e-learning are most readily available for educational purposes within organisations, and can be found in 73 per cent of organisations. These were followed by generic and customised modules. Less readily available, but still used, were web-mediated person-to-person communications, including what are termed 'asynchronous' web discussions, or web forums supported by organisations, and 'synchronous' web seminars delivered by a subject expert.

Increasingly, online learning is occurring in the home and now ranks at a higher proportion than online learning occurring in educational establishments and learning centres. It is suggested that this may reflect the failure of educational institutions to as yet fully embrace new learning technologies.

And finally...

Recent research by the Institute for Public Policy Research showed that UK children spend on average half of their spare time watching TV, playing video games and surfing the Internet. It was not clear how much of these activities was devoted to educational content.

⇨ Information from the Economic and Social Research Council. Visit www.esrc.ac.uk for more information.
© Economic and Social Research Council

Studying at UK universities

Frequently asked questions

Why should I go to university? What are the benefits?

Higher education provides many benefits for the individual, including enhanced career prospects and often increased earning potential, as well as wider cultural, social and economic benefits. The Department for Education and Skills gives an overview of some of these on its website.

> **Higher education provides many benefits for the individual, including enhanced career prospects and often increased earning potential**

Is there a list of undergraduate/ postgraduate courses in the UK?

Undergraduate courses: The Universities & Colleges Admissions Service (UCAS) annually publishes a comprehensive guide to undergraduate courses in the UK, available both in hard copy and online. The Education UK website also contains a complete UK undergraduate course database. ECCTIS, a private consortium, manages the UK's national courses database, owned by the Department for Education and Skills.

Postgraduate courses: Graduate Prospects (the commercial subsidiary of the Higher Education Careers Services Unit (CSU)) publishes the Prospects postgraduate database (covering taught and research degrees) online.

Higher Education Research Opportunities in the United Kingdom (HERO) also provides information

about courses and individual universities publish their own prospectuses.

I need a list of universities and colleges in the…(e.g. North-West) region. Can you send me one?

Higher Education Research Opportunities in the United Kingdom (HERO) and the Universities & Colleges Admissions Service (UCAS) both provide maps of all UK universities and colleges that provide higher education. HERO's website also includes a breakdown of universities by region.

What are the different qualifications awarded by a university?

The range of courses and qualifications on offer at UK universities is very broad. There are three main levels: Bachelor's, Master's and Doctoral. Foundation degrees are also being introduced. The Quality Assurance Agency (QAA) provides a guide to help explain the different levels of qualifications.

What is the applications process to study at university?

All information on how and when

to apply to undergraduate courses is available on the Universities & Colleges Admissions Service (UCAS) website. Go to their 'how to apply' section for more information.

Information about applying for postgraduate courses, as well as online application forms, are available too.

How do I know if the admissions system is fair?

Institutions work hard to ensure that their admissions procedures are fair and transparent. For many popular courses there may be more suitably-qualified applicants than there are places available, so each year some applicants may be disappointed in not being admitted to their first choice of university. The final decision on any individual's application is a matter for the individual institution.

What qualifications do I need to get into university?

The requirements vary depending on the course. Most UK students will need two or more A levels or equivalent. The Universities & Colleges Admissions Service

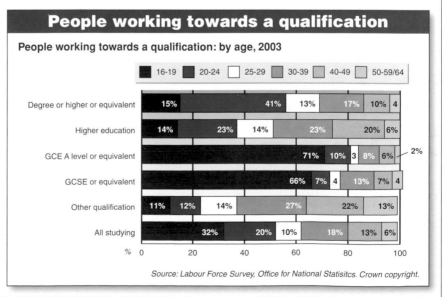

People working towards a qualification

People working towards a qualification: by age, 2003

	16-19	20-24	25-29	30-39	40-49	50-59/64
Degree or higher or equivalent	15%		41%	13%	17%	10% 4
Higher education	14%	23%	14%	23%	20%	6%
GCE A level or equivalent		71%	10% 3	8%	6%	2%
GCSE or equivalent		66%	7% 4	13%	7%	4
Other qualification	11%	12%	14%	27%	22%	13%
All studying	32%	20%	10%	18%	13%	6%

% 0   20   40   60   80   100

Source: Labour Force Survey, Office for National Statisitcs. Crown copyright.

(UCAS) provides entry profiles for the different courses, giving information about the types and grade of qualification that may be accepted.

Which universities provide courses in X?

You can find out by doing a course search on the Universities & Colleges Admissions Service (UCAS) website. A list of institutions offering the course will be shown when you select what you want to study.

Which A levels/qualifications are required for a particular course?

For undergraduate courses, this information is available from the Universities & Colleges Admissions Service (UCAS).

The range of courses and qualifications on offer at UK universities is very broad

---

Do a course search online and once you have found the course you want to study click on 'entry profile for this course'. Often the entry requirements are expressed as a 'tariff' or points score. UCAS has a tariff calculator that can be used to find out if you've got the right qualifications.

What's Clearing and how does it work?

Clearing is a service provided by the Universities & Colleges Admissions Service (UCAS) for students who may not have obtained the grades they require for their conditional offer; did not receive or have not accepted any offers; or who decided to apply to university late, after applications had closed; or after getting their results. It matches appropriately-qualified students with those universities and colleges who have places available. More information can be found on their website.

How can a mature student find out if they're qualified to start a course?

Admission requirements vary but

are often more flexible for mature students to reflect their experience in other areas. A range of qualifications is accepted, and for students without the A levels, GNVQs, O levels, or GCSEs that may be required, universities offer various access courses as a way in. Contact the relevant admissions tutor for more information. The Universities & Colleges Admissions Service (UCAS) publishes a comprehensive guide to HE for mature students. Information is also available from the Department for Education and Skills and Higher Education Research Opportunities in the United Kingdom (HERO).

What's an access course?

Access programmes aim to prepare adult learners and those without the traditional HE entry qualifications for admission to undergraduate education. A significant number of students entering Higher Education now do so from access programmes. For more information about the courses available please visit the Universities & and Colleges Admissions Service (UCAS) website.

How can an international student find out if their qualifications are valid to study in the UK or how their qualification compares to its English equivalent?

You can check the equivalence of your country's qualifications with those in the UK by contacting the National Academic Recognition Information Centre for the United Kingdom (UK NARIC), which runs an information service for international students.

In addition, the Department for Education and Skills; the Council for International Education; Higher Education Research Opportunities in the United Kingdom (HERO) and the British Council all provide information for international students.

Are there any websites that provide information about studying in the UK for international students?

The Council for International Education (UKCOSA) provides guidance for international students as does the Department for Education and Skills.

Where can EU students find out more about studying in the UK?

The Department for Education and Skills provides comprehensive information and advice for EU students, including a frequently asked questions section.

Last updated: 26 April 2006

⇨ The above information is reprinted with kind permission from Universities UK. Visit www.universitiesuk.ac.uk for more.

© *Universities UK*

Undergraduate applicants up 6.4% for 2007

Information from UCAS

The number of people applying to full-time undergraduate courses at UK universities and colleges has increased by 6.4%, latest statistics from UCAS show. The rise represents 395,307 applicants applying to enter HE in 2007 compared to 371,683 in 2006. The snapshot of data is taken at UCAS' 15 January advisory closing date for UK and EU applicants, although it is possible to apply right up until the start of the academic year.

Anthony McClaran, UCAS Chief Executive, said: 'These figures are encouraging for all who believe the expansion of higher education is good for individuals and good for our society. Not only has last year's dip in applications been reversed, but application levels are now higher than in 2005 which had previously broken all records. The increase is particularly marked in England.

'It's also good to see evidence of effective competition for international students, with double-digit increases in the key markets of India, Pakistan and the United States.'

'These figures are encouraging for all who believe the expansion of higher education is good for individuals and good for our society'

Applicants from England increased by 7.1% to 291,075 from 271,663. Applicants from other UK nations showed a 0.1% fall in those from Wales, a 0.9% rise in Scottish applicants and a 3.0% fall in applicants from Northern Ireland. The Northern Ireland fall equates to 484 applicants.

Applicants to English universities and colleges increased by 7.2%, to Scottish institutions by 1.9%, and to Northern Ireland by 0.3% and those applying to Welsh institutions fell by 0.1%.

The number of people applying from outside of the EU is up 6.6% from 22,105 to 23,570. Applicants from China have risen by 1.3% and Hong Kong 10.3%. Amongst the other countries contributing the largest number of non-EU applicants were the United States (up 12.3%), Malaysia (up 4.7%), Pakistan (up 19.1%), Singapore (up 9.5%) and India (up 13.8%).

Those choosing to defer one or more of their choices for a year fell from 23,354 last year to 22,656 this year. 5.8% of applicant's choices were made for deferred entry this year, compared with 6.4% in 2006.
14 February 2007

⇨ The above information is reprinted with kind permission from UCAS. Visit www.ucas.ac.uk for more information.

© UCAS

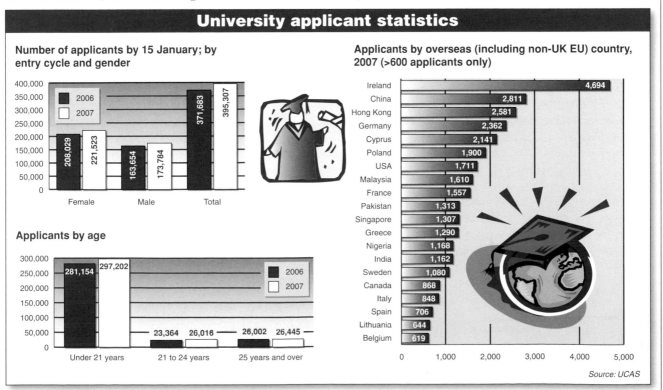

University applicant statistics

Number of applicants by 15 January; by entry cycle and gender

	Female	Male	Total
2006	208,029	163,654	371,683
2007	221,523	173,784	395,307

Applicants by age

	Under 21 years	21 to 24 years	25 years and over
2006	281,154	23,364	26,002
2007	297,202	26,016	26,445

Applicants by overseas (including non-UK EU) country, 2007 (>600 applicants only)

Country	Applicants
Ireland	4,694
China	2,811
Hong Kong	2,581
Germany	2,362
Cyprus	2,141
Poland	1,900
USA	1,711
Malaysia	1,610
France	1,557
Pakistan	1,313
Singapore	1,307
Greece	1,290
Nigeria	1,168
India	1,162
Sweden	1,080
Canada	868
Italy	848
Spain	706
Lithuania	644
Belgium	619

Source: UCAS

Student numbers and statistics

Frequently asked questions

How many HE students are there in the UK?

In 2004/05, there were approximately 2.3 million students in the UK (Total undergraduate and postgraduate).

England: approx. 1.9 million; Wales: approx. 125,000; Scotland: approx. 210,000; Northern Ireland: approx. 55,000.

Source: Higher Education Statistics Agency (HESA) (2005): Students in Higher Education Institutions 2004/05, table 0a

How many people apply for university each year?

A total of 390,890 students were accepted onto undergraduate courses through Universities & Colleges Admissions Service (UCAS) for the academic year 2006/07, of which approx. 345,564 were home applicants. *Source: UCAS 2006/07*

What proportion of 17- to 30-year-olds currently enter higher education?

The Department for Education and Skills estimated that in 2003/04, approximately 43 per cent of UK 17- to 30-year-olds currently enter HE. *Source: Department for Education and Skills (DfES) (2005): SFR 14/2005*

What proportion of under-21s enter higher education?

Across the UK an average of 35 per cent of under-21s enter HE (2001/02). This figure for Scotland was 50 per cent for 2002/03 and 44 per cent in Northern Ireland in 2003/04. *Source: Department for Education and Skills (DfES), Scottish Executive, Department of Education Northern Ireland (DENI)*

What proportion of undergraduates are women/men?

In 2003/04, approximately 58 per cent of undergraduate students are women and 42 per cent were men. *Source: Higher Education Statistics Agency (HESA) (2005): Students in Higher Education Institutions 2003/04, table 1*

What proportion of first-year undergraduates are mature students?

52 per cent of first-year undergraduate students are mature students (i.e. 21 years of age and older when starting to study). *Source: Higher Education Statistics Agency (HESA) (2005): Students in Higher Education Institutions 2003/04, tables 1b, 1f*

What proportion of students study in each subject area?

1 Medicine & dentistry 2.4%
2 Subjects allied to medicine 12.8%
3 Biological sciences 6.6%
4 Veterinary science 0.2%
5 Agriculture & related subjects 0.7%
6 Physical sciences 3.3%
7 Mathematical sciences 1.4%
8 Computer science 6.1%
9 Engineering & technology 6.0%
10 Architecture, building & planning 2.1%
11 Social studies 8.5%
12 Law 3.7%
13 Business and administrative studies 13.4%
14 Mass communications & documentation 2.0%
15 Languages 6.0%
16 Historical and philosophical studies 4.5%
17 Creative arts and design 6.2%
18 Education 8.6%
19 Combined 5.5%

Source: Higher Education Statistics Agency (HESA) (2005): Students in Higher Education Institutions 2003/04, tables 2a-d

How many EU students (excluding UK students) are studying in UK universities?

In 2003/04 there were approximately 90,000 students from EU countries (excluding the UK). *Source: Higher Education Statistics Agency (HESA) (2005): Students in Higher Education Institutions 2003/04, table 1*

How many (non-EU) international students are there in the UK?

In 2003/04 there were approximately 211,000 students from non-EU countries. *Source: Higher Education Statistics Agency (HESA) (2005): Students in Higher Education Institutions 2003/04, table 1*

Last updated: 16 March 2007

⇨ Universities UK is the representative body for the executive heads of UK universities. It works to advance the interests of universities and to spread good practice throughout the higher education sector. Visit www.universitiesuk.ac.uk for more information.

© Universities UK

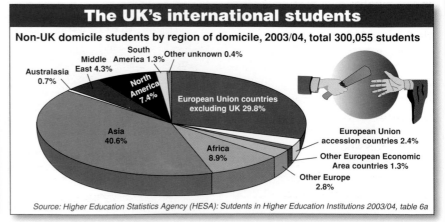

The UK's international students

Non-UK domicile students by region of domicile, 2003/04, total 300,055 students

- South America 1.3%
- Other unknown 0.4%
- Middle East 4.3%
- Australasia 0.7%
- North America 7.4%
- European Union countries excluding UK 29.8%
- Asia 40.6%
- Africa 8.9%
- European Union accession countries 2.4%
- Other European Economic Area countries 1.3%
- Other Europe 2.8%

Source: Higher Education Statistics Agency (HESA): Sutdents in Higher Education Institutions 2003/04, table 6a

Alarm as students achieve record top degrees

By Graeme Paton, Education Correspondent

Two out of three university students graduated with a top degree last year, according to figures certain to raise fresh concerns that standards are in decline.

The Higher Education Statistics Agency revealed that a record 172,000 students (60 per cent) gained a first- or upper-second-class degree last summer – 6,700 more than in the previous year. Of those awarded a top degree, 34,800 gained a first and 137,200 an upper-second.

The figures represent a rise of one per cent on 2005 and numbers have continued to climb over the last decade. In 1996, only 48 per cent of students left university with a top degree. Of those, seven per cent were awarded a first against 12 per cent in 2006.

In all, 316,000 students completed degree courses in 2006. There were 26,800 who failed with an 'unclassified' result.

But even such good degrees might not secure the best jobs at a time when fears are growing that the employment market is being swamped.

A survey of the 100 top employers of graduates, which included BT, Google, HSBC and Tesco, found that they expected 50 applicants for each job and the leading investment banks anticipated up to 300 applicants.

Martin Birchall, the managing director of High Fliers Research, which carried out the survey, published today, said: 'The growth in the number of graduate jobs has not kept pace with the enormous rise in the number of people going to university over the last decade.

'It has been Government policy for a number of years now to increase further the number of school-leavers going to university – but that is simply going to add to the tens of thousands of graduates who do not have jobs to match their qualifications.'

Good news for graduates, according to his survey, is that those who do get jobs can expect average starting salaries to reach £25,500 – £1,700 more than last year.

Mr Birchall said that leading employers were still concentrating their recruitment drives on an elite group of 10 or 20 top universities, with Manchester, Cambridge and Nottingham being the most sought after by employers.

But the figures from the Higher Education Statistics Agency are certain to revive doubts about the quality of degrees.

Two out of three university students graduated with a top degree last year

A Government-backed working group, led by Bob Burgess, the vice-chancellor of Leicester University, concluded last year that the present classification system was not 'fit for purpose'.

It recommended the adoption of a new system in which students gain a pass or fail, along with a detailed transcript of their achievements.

Last month, Bangor University was accused of lowering its academic standards with a proposal to boost the number of first-class degrees.

A leaked document written by its pro vice-chancellor said that its nearest rival, Aberystwyth, awarded more first- and upper-second-class degrees and it had to 'redress the balance with all expedition'.

Peter Williams, of the Quality Assurance Agency, an independent university watchdog, said: 'The problem with the present system is that it was designed at another time, for another purpose and a different kind of student population. With so many students now in the system, it no longer provides us with useful information about a graduate's ability.'

This week's HESA figures also revealed a two per cent increase in the number of students enrolling on undergraduate and postgraduate courses in 2005-06, to 2,336,100.

Bill Rammell, the higher education minister, hailed the rise, saying: 'The underlying trend is still up and the proportions of applicants from lower socio-economic groups has not fallen. I am hopeful that the application figures for 2007-08 will continue this positive trend.'

12 January 2007

Funding options

Higher education doesn't come cheap. TheSite.org outlines your main funding options

This is a simple guide outlining the different sources of funding for undergraduates. It's worth finding out about all of them. You may not be eligible for every scheme, but if you don't ask, you don't get.

What's the cost?

In 2006, university fees will rise to a maximum of £3,000 per year. Full-time undergraduate students don't have to pay these fees while they're studying. As detailed below, a loan scheme operates for all UK-based students – who have been registered residents for a minimum of three years – while some may find further grants and dispensations are available.

Student loans

This is the name for a financial support package from the government, offering loans to help all students with their living fees. These are means-tested (which means an assessment is made based on your finances) and eventually have to be repaid – plus interest linked to the rate of inflation. The key is that you don't have to begin repayments until you're in work and earning an annual salary of £15,000 and above.

Loans are organised by the Student Loans Company, but you start by

contacting your Award Authority, which is governed by a different body depending on where you live:

You don't have to begin student loan repayments until you're in work and earning an annual salary of £15,000 and above

---

⇨ England – apply through your Local Education Authority, or by visiting www.studentsupportdirect.co.uk/
⇨ Wales – apply through your Local Education Authority, or by visiting www.studentfinancewales.co.uk
⇨ Scotland – apply through the Student Awards Agency for Scotland, or by visiting www.student-support-saas.gov.uk
⇨ Northern Ireland – apply through your Education and Library

Board, or by visiting http://www.delni.gov.uk/

Alternatively, you can apply online at: www.studentfinancedirect.co.uk

For a guide to the maximum loan amount available, depending on your financial cirucmstances, visit Support 4 Learning's loan section.

Parental contribution

A large proportion of students have to rely on their parents to pay for university fees and some of their subsistence money. Parents are given a suggested amount for their contribution, but unfortunately it cannot be legally enforced.

Higher education grant

Students coming from a family with an income under £15,200 are entitled to apply for a grant of up to £1,000. You do not have to pay this back. Smaller grants are also available, if your family income is under £21,185.

For other sources of cash to get you through your student days, check our extra funding options at TheSite.org.

⇨ The above information is reprinted with kind permission from TheSite.org. Visit www.thesite.org for more information.

© *TheSite.org*

GOODBYE, GOOD LUCK!

The cost of a degree

New students expect to pay £33,512 to get a degree

With exam results and the new university fee structure on the horizon, the 2006 NatWest Student Money Matters survey reveals that sixth formers starting university this year expect to pay £33,512 for a three-year degree course. This is up from £28,600 last year and includes the new tuition fees. As a result, they expect to graduate with £14,779 of debt, an increase of £1,099 on 2005 figures.

Despite these figures, however, 79% of 2006's intake believe that going to university will help them with their future job prospects and 53% wanted to use the opportunity to train for a specific career such as medicine or law.

Level of graduate debt slowing

Graduate debt continues to rise, although at a much slower pace to previous years. Graduates now leave university with £13,252 of debt, an increase of £612 (5%) on 2005. That said, the percentage of graduates leaving university with debts of over £10,000 remained the same as in 2005 at 62%.

The average starting salary has fallen this year from £14,090 in 2005 to £13,860 in 2006, however, on the other hand, more graduates (23%) did have a job confirmed on graduation (up from 18% in 2005). Again despite lower starting salaries, 56% of graduates admit that they have landed a good job, 41% are now totally independent from their parents and 43% claim to have a healthier bank balance (up from 28% in 2005).

Just over half (57%) of the students questioned admitted to being concerned about the amount of debt that they were in. However, only 22% (down from 29% in 2005) had actually considered packing it all in to pursue a full-time job.

For sixth formers starting university this summer, the biggest concern was money being tight (71%). Worrying about finances continued to outweigh concerns about the educational aspects of university by 11%, as 60% were concerned about failing their exams or keeping up to date with the workload (59%).

Massive increase in part-time workers

Students are now increasingly relying on part-time jobs to finance their life at university. A massive 87% of this year's intake believe that they will have to get a part-time job and 46% of current students have to rely on their income from term-time work to get by, working an average of 14 hours a week. Current students supplement their income by an average of £71.32 per week. The pressure of having to earn money continues to have an impact on students' studies, with 31% admitting they had skipped lectures because of their part-time job, although this figure is down significantly on those respondents in 2005.

Parents footing the bill

Despite debt increasing and part-time work becoming a necessity, the good news is that two-thirds of parents finance their children's university education. 28% give regular amounts throughout the term, 26% get money from their parents as and when they need it, 8% get a lump sum at the beginning of each term and 4% got a one-off amount when they started university.

Mark Worthington, Head of NatWest Student and Graduate Banking, said: 'New students are clearly much more clued up about the financial realities of university than in previous years. Despite the anticipated cost of university rising by 17% on 2005, students are taking it in their stride and cutting back on their spending, meaning they only expect to graduate with 8% more debt than those not paying the increased tuition fees.

'University really plays a huge part in shaping a person's future. It not only gives them the educational background needed to really succeed in the world of business but it teaches them valuable life lessons that enable them to stand on their own two feet successfully.'

To help students understand the change to university funding and how it affects them, NatWest has developed a handy guide to student finance. The guide covers Government Support and the finance available from banks and the Student Loans Company and aims to remove confusion around the financial aspects of university for parents and students alike.

15 August 2006

⇨ The above information is reprinted with kind permission from NatWest. Visit www.natwest.com for more information.

© *NatWest*

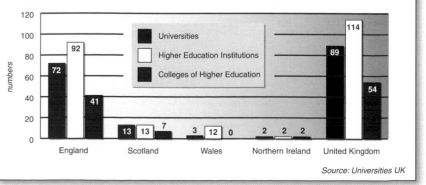

Number of higher education institutions

How many universities and higher education institutions are there in the UK? (Plus breakdown by England, Wales, Scotland, Ireland.) Number of institutions (as at August 2006)

Source: Universities UK

Slow growth in graduate starting salaries

Slow growth in graduate starting salaries leaves many deferring life decisions and wishing they had done a business or science degree

One-third of graduates feel they did the wrong course, and many feel the costs and related debts are stopping them from buying a house, starting a family and saving for retirement six years after they graduated. These are some of the findings from a new survey that explores the impact of tuition fees and looks at what organisations must do to attract and retain graduates, from the Chartered Institute of Personnel and Development (CIPD).

Photo: Gisela Royo

The new survey – *Graduates in the workplace – does a degree add value?* – finds that 23% of those who graduated in 2005 that would choose a different course would opt for a more scientific/technical course and 22% would choose a business-based course or a professional qualification.

Victoria Winkler, CIPD Learning, Training and Development Adviser, says: 'A combination of fierce competition for graduate jobs and graduates taking longer to find work appears to be having an impact on their views about their choice of degree. The findings show that with reflection many graduates would study a subject that relates directly to business or that will better equip them with skills that are transferable into the workplace. However, most graduates value their time at university, and would still go to university if they had their time again.

'These findings suggest that the Government needs to work alongside employers to find out what skills are needed in the workplace. This information then needs to be fed into schools and colleges so that school leavers have the information needed to make a more informed decision about the course they choose to study and their future career.'

Finance

⇨ The increase in average starting salaries between those who graduated in 2000 and 2005 is just 8%, with those graduating in 2005 earning a mean starting salary of £19,451 and 2000 graduates starting with a mean of £18,016.

⇨ One-third of those who graduated in 2005 are failing to contribute to a pensions saving scheme. And despite receiving a rapid increase in salary once they are working – year 2000 graduates have seen their salary increase by an average 55% to a mean current salary of £27,879 – one-fifth of those who graduated in 2000 still fail to contribute to a pension.

John Philpott, CIPD Chief Economist, says: 'The increase in starting salaries over the last five years is well below the increase in both retail price inflation and average earnings during the same period. A combination of the drop in starting salaries, slightly weaker labour market conditions and increased inflation makes it much more difficult for many new graduates to get a foot on the property ladder and to start saving for retirement.

'The rapid increase in salary once graduates are working enables them to start to repay debt and gain a foothold on the housing ladder. But the obvious temptation will be to devote whatever disposable income is left after meeting debt repayments and essential living costs to lifestyle spending – socialising, holidays – rather than saving for the future. But in doing this graduates are failing to save for the future and their wish to retire in their early sixties looks doubtful.'

Female graduates at a disadvantage

⇨ The gender pay gap has doubled since 2001 – men graduating in 2005 earn a starting salary that is 14% more than the average woman graduating in 2005.

⇨ Just 57% of women graduating in 2005 contribute to a pension scheme compared to 70% of men.

⇨ Women who graduated in 2005 are 12 times more likely to believe that gender is holding them back in their career than men.

'Women are more likely to take time out of work to have children and work part-time which means many will be contributing less to pension investments than men. This makes it even more important for women to start contributing to pension investments early on, however, almost half of women who graduated in 2005 are failing to make any contribution to pension funds. This could leave many women unable to make the necessary contribution to pension investments in order to retire at the same age as men,' adds Victoria Winkler.

Graduates value time at university

➪ Over 90% of respondents, regardless of when they graduated, state they would go to university if they had their time again.

➪ 84% of respondents graduating in 2005 state their time at university has been most helpful in terms of gaining independence and better life skills.

➪ 74% of respondents graduating in 2005 feel that going to university has given them the opportunity to earn a higher wage.

➪ 69% of respondents graduating in 2005 believe it has helped with career progression.

➪ Around three-quarters (64%) of respondents graduating in 2005 believe it has helped with the skills and ability required to do the job.

➪ Around three-quarters of graduates indicate that their time at university has been helpful in terms of communication skills, presentation skills, team-work and confidence.

18 December 2006

➪ The above information is reprinted with kind permission from the Chartered Institute of Personnel and Development. Please visit their website at www.cipd.co.uk for more information.

© Chartered Institute of Personnel and Development

A fortune by degrees

The courses that could earn you £300,000 more

By Laura Clark, Education Reporter

It is a sum that could prompt potential students to consider their subject choices very carefully.

The earning power of a degree is today shown to vary by more than £300,000 depending on the discipline studied at university.

Science and engineering graduates tend to be the biggest earners, with medics bringing in an extra £340,315 during their working lives.

In contrast, over their careers arts graduates earn on average only an additional £34,494 than classmates with just A levels.

There is even evidence to suggest men with arts degrees would be wealthier if they had given university a miss altogether.

For the average graduate, additional gross earnings over a lifetime are calculated at £160,061 – significantly less than the £400,000 figure trumpeted by the Government as justification for raising tuition fees to £3,000 a year.

Even ministers now accept the sum wildly overestimates the earning power of a degree.

Universities UK, which commissioned the PricewaterhouseCoopers research, said the new figure was 'the most accurate we think we can get'.

But the university bosses' group pointed out that the £160,000 earnings figure – which gives £120,000 after tax – was still 20 to 25 per cent higher than those with just A levels.

The research by PricewaterhouseCoopers does not break down graduate earnings by sex. However, a Warwick University study cited in the report did examine the gender gap – and found a negative earnings premium for male arts graduate.

For women, it was positive but still lower than for all other disciplines.

For today's report, analysts used data from nearly a million workers to calculate graduates' lifetime earnings compared with those whose highest qualifications are A levels.

They came up with figures varying between £340,315 extra for medicine and dentistry and £34,494 for arts subjects, which include design, fine art and drama.

However, these sums fail to take into account the actual cost of doing a degree – the lost earning opportunities during the period of study and the amount paid in tuition fees.

Figures for the overall 'rate of return' suggest that law students reap the biggest rewards for their investment, at 17.2 per cent per year, closely followed by those who studied management, on 16.9 per cent. The average is 12.1 per cent.

The research, conducted in association with the London Economics consultancy, also claimed a surge in the number of graduates over the past 20 years had failed to dent the earnings premium.

This was because demand for graduates had risen in tandem with their increased numbers.

The report also concluded that a university education was linked with a range of non-financial benefits – including lower rates of obesity and depression.

Diana Warwick, chief executive of Universities UK, said: 'Higher education is still clearly a worthwhile investment for the individual.'

➪ This article first appeared in the *Daily Mail*, 7 February 2007.

© 2007 Associated Newspapers Ltd

The graduate gap

Gross additional lifetime earnings by degree subject compared with two or more A levels

Medicine	£340,315
Engineering	£243,730
Maths/computer sciences	£241,749
Environmental/physical sciences	£237,935
Architecture	£195,297
Business	£184,694
Social sciences including law	£169,267
AVERAGE DEGREE	**£160,061**
Biosciences	£111,269
European languages	£96,281
Humanities	£51,549
Arts	£34,494

Male stereotypes barrier to university entrance

Information from the Institute of Education, University of London

Stereotypical attitudes to being male could be an obstacle to men taking up university studies, finds new research from the Institute of Education.

A team led by Dr Penny Jane Burke interviewed 38 mainly working-class men aged 18 to 54 on courses preparing them for university study. They found that the men feared that they would not be able to overcome their natural tendency to 'ladishness' and what they saw as male laziness and lack of organisation.

Yet the men also had high aspirations and saw a degree as the key to gaining respectability and becoming 'a real man', finds the Economic and Social Research Council-funded study. This is defined as being the breadwinner, with a good income and a successful career, and having symbols of success including a wife, family, car and house.

The men came from a range of ethnic backgrounds – only three were white, working-class British. Though all were classed as 'home' students, some had migrated to the UK from other countries and had suffered traumatic life experiences. Many were dependent on their families to support their time away from paid work.

The men tended to doubt their own ability and value. They explained their past educational underachievement in terms of inborn laziness and saw this as the key obstacle to getting into and doing well at university. Although many were skilled and experienced – some came from professional backgrounds in their own countries – they were afraid they wouldn't be able to write essays and were anxious that potential failure would expose them to ridicule and confirm their self-doubts.

But they were also eager to achieve, meet the expectations of their family and ethnic communities and use education to improve themselves.

Dr Burke comments: 'Emphasising supposed natural male abilities or deficiencies over the need to study, manage one's time and develop skills not necessarily seen as men's domain could deter many men from aiming for university.

'These men have high hopes but have to overcome their own and others' assumptions that boys and men are naturally lazy and unable to be as organised as girls and women.'
12 July 2006

⇨ The above information is reprinted with kind permission from the Institute of Education, University of London. Visit www.ioe.ac.uk for more information.
© *Institute of Education, University of London*

'Mickey Mouse' degrees come of age

From surfing to brewing beer: 'Mickey Mouse' courses have come of age, says university body

⇨ *Wide range of degrees helps diversity, says report*
⇨ *Higher education working closely with employers*

They have been derided as Mickey Mouse degrees, with little academic merit. But qualifications such as surf science and technology are riding the crest of the economic wave, according to Universities UK.

Degrees in computer games technology, golf management, brewing and distilling, and cosmetic science are among those flourishing, says

By James Meikle, education correspondent

the group that represents Britain's universities, in a report aimed at proving how closely higher education is working with employers to provide vocational skills.

Drummond Bone, president of Universities UK, said courses once

described as 'Mickey Mouse' were now the 'mouse that roared'. 'If our graduates are to take their place in the global economy, it is right that there should be a range of courses on offer to ensure a workforce with diverse, and in some cases very specific, skills.'

The report says graduate-level jobs in the computer industry, already worth £65.5bn a year to the economy, are expected to jump 20% to 530,000 by 2014. Those in the £310bn financial services sector will rise by an eighth to 450,000 and in the £90bn media and fashion industry by a 12th to nearly 1.6m. Demand for graduates in the £10bn sport and leisure industry is expected to soar beyond the present 53,000 and better-qualified white-collar staff are urgently needed in the construction industry, which employs 2 million people.

Courses at 26 universities are singled out in the report, including a Master's degree in computing run jointly by Sussex University and American Express and an accountancy degree course run by Ernst and Young with Lancaster University.

They have been derided as Mickey Mouse degrees, with little academic merit. But qualifications such as surf science and technology are riding the crest of the economic wave, according to Universities UK

Ministers are demanding employers improve links with higher education and want more vocational courses to be created. The government is introducing new powers for further education colleges to offer foundation degrees, equivalent to about two years of a traditional three-year undergraduate degree in England, in an effort to spur competition.

Lord Leitch, who is heading an inquiry for the chancellor, Gordon Brown, into the skills needed in Britain by 2020, is expected next month to praise higher education's contribution but to say that Britain's 26% of adults with degrees is only just over the average for the 'rich man's club' of the Organisation for Economic Cooperation and Development.

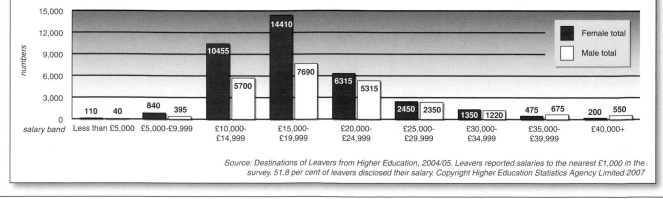

Alan Johnson, the education secretary, says in the foreword to the report that 'as the HE sector begins to operate in a more competitive market, employer-led provision will enable delivery of the skills that the labour market needs and that students want'.

Richard Lambert, the director-general of the CBI, said the courses highlighted in the report 'need to be celebrated and encouraged'. But Sally Hunt, joint general secretary of the University and College Union, warned last night: 'Universities are not just about providing degrees based on what business is right for the country or only providing courses that make profit or appear the most popular.'

The surf science and technology degree that started in 1999 at Plymouth University 'got the usual sniggers' even among academics, said Malcolm Findlay, who helped set the course, but they soon became less dismissive. 'Even if students do not surf very well, they do get an understanding of physics, biomechanics and the physiology that goes with it.'

Degree of difference
Cosmetic science
A London Metropolitan University degree developed in consultation with Elizabeth Arden
Voluntary sector management
First aid, transport and care are taught in Derby University's foundation degree developed with St John Ambulance
Golf management studies
An applied degree at Birmingham University established with the Professional Golfers' Association
Computer games technology
Degree course at Abertay Dundee University
Brewing and distilling
Degrees and diplomas at Heriot-Watt University in Edinburgh
28 November 2006
© *Guardian Newspapers Limited 2007*

Destination of higher education leavers

UK-domiciled leavers who obtained first-degree qualifications and entered or continued in full-time UK employment by salary band and gender, 2004/05

salary band	Less than £5,000	£5,000-£9,999	£10,000-£14,999	£15,000-£19,999	£20,000-£24,999	£25,000-£29,999	£30,000-£34,999	£35,000-£39,999	£40,000+
Female total	110	840	10455	14410	6315	2450	1350	475	200
Male total	40	395	5700	7690	5315	2350	1220	675	550

Source: Destinations of Leavers from Higher Education, 2004/05. Leavers reported salaries to the nearest £1,000 in the survey. 51.8 per cent of leavers disclosed their salary. Copyright Higher Education Statistics Agency Limited 2007

Issues

www.independence.co.uk

⇨ In the UK in 2004/5 there were 9,963,000 school pupils. Public sector schools were attended by 92 per cent (9.2 million) of pupils, while seven per cent attended one of the 2,500 non-maintained mainstream schools. (page 1)

⇨ The participation rates for 16-year-olds who continue in post-compulsory education and training is 73 per cent. This number is made up of 78 per cent females and 68 per cent males. (page 2)

⇨ The country with the highest expenditure on education is Denmark, at 8.3% of its GDP (gross dometic product). The lowest is Japan, at only 3.7%. The UK spends 5.4% of its GDP on education. (page 3)

⇨ Pupils achieving top grades at GCSE rise year by year. 45.4% of pupils achieved five or more grades A* to C at GCSE in academic year 1995/96. In 2004/05, this figure was 57%. (page 3)

⇨ The Learning and Skills Council is responsible for funding and planning education and training for over-16-year-olds in England. (page 4)

⇨ Pupils like variety. They want to learn through a variety of approaches, including teacher-supported and self-directed learning. Older pupils in particular like some individual responsibility and autonomy in their learning. (page 7)

⇨ In 2003/04 pupils from Black Caribbean, Other Black and Mixed White and Black Caribbean groups were among the most likely to be permanently excluded from schools in England. (page 8)

⇨ Girls generally perform better than boys at GCSE and at GCE A level (or equivalent) in the UK. In 2004/05, 62 per cent of girls in their last year of compulsory education achieved five or more GCSE grades A* to C, compared with 52 per cent of boys. (page 10)

⇨ While girls are now achieving better academic results than boys at age 16, relatively few young women are choosing science or science-related subjects for further study. (page 11)

⇨ Single-sex education brought almost no advantage in terms of exam results. Girls from girls' schools did only slightly better in exams than their co-educational peers. Boys did no better at all. (page 12)

⇨ Recent research suggests that education policy by itself contributes little to the rate at which people move between social classes. (page 13)

⇨ Most academies have made good progress in improving GCSE results, and the programme is on track to deliver good value for money. (page 15)

⇨ More than half of secondary school teachers in England and Wales (53%) do not think that setting up city academies is an appropriate way of raising standards in deprived areas. (page 16)

⇨ Around a fifth of employers often find non-graduate recruits of all ages have literacy or numeracy problems, yet a third expect the levels of skills required for work will increase over the next five years. (page 17)

⇨ 70% of students believe that it is harder to get an A grade at A level in science-based subjects compared to 'softer' subjects. (page 21)

⇨ When questioned about their past exam experiences, 57% of UK adults received better results than they were expecting. (page 22)

⇨ The proportion of 16-year-olds staying on in full-time education in the UK is below the average for developed countries. (page 26)

⇨ The Open University, which teaches by distance learning, is the largest university in the UK. In 2004/5 it had over 173,000 students, making it three times the size of the next largest UK university. (page 28)

⇨ The number of people applying to full-time undergraduate courses at UK universities and colleges has increased by 6.4%, latest statistics from UCAS show. (page 31)

⇨ 29.8% of the UK's international students come from EU countries (excluding the UK). (page 32)

⇨ Two out of three university students graduated with a top degree in 2006. (page 33)

⇨ Graduate debt continues to rise, although at a much slower pace to previous years. Graduates now leave university with £13,252 of debt, an increase of £612 (5%) on 2005. (page 35)

⇨ One-third of graduates feel they did the wrong course, and many feel the costs and related debts are stopping them from buying a house, starting a family and saving for retirement six years after they graduate. (page 36)

⇨ The earning power of a degree is today shown to vary by more than £300,000 depending on the discipline studied at university. (page 37)

GLOSSARY

A levels
This stands for Advanced level. These are qualifications usually taken by students aged 16 to 18 at schools and sixth form colleges, although they can be taken at any time by school leavers at local colleges or through distance learning. They provide an accepted route to degree courses and university and usually take two years to complete. Once you have passed the AS level in a subject, you can opt to study in more depth by taking the second half of the A-level course known as A2.

Academies
Sometimes called city academies, academies are a government initiative to improve educational standards in disadvantaged areas. They are independent state schools, either brand new or built to replace a failing school. They are set up as charitable companies by business, faith or voluntary groups and receive both sponsorship from that group and government funding.

AS levels
This stands for Advanced Supplementary level, which is equivalent to half an A level. They can either be studied as the first half of an A level or as a qualification in their own right. They usually take one year to complete.

Co-educational schools
This refers to schools which have a mix of both boys and girls, as opposed to single-sex schools, which do not. Most students in the UK attend co-educational schools, although some people feel that single-sex schools provide a better learning environment.

GCSEs
GCSE stands for General Certificate of Secondary Education. These are studied at school during years 10 and 11 and usually sat in year 11, although school leavers can choose to take GCSEs at any time at a local college or through distance learning. Most year 11 students will sit between eight and 11 GCSEs in different subjects, and some subjects, including maths and English, are compulsory.

GNVQs
This stands for General National Vocational Qualification. These are intended for young people aged 16 to 19 who are in full-time education, and offer a vocational alternative to traditional academic qualifications.

Graduate
Someone who is educated to degree level.

Highers and Advanced Highers
These are the Scottish equivalent of AS and A levels, taken in the last two years of school respectively and providing a route into university. Unlike AS levels, however, the Higher grade does not count towards the Advanced Higher grade.

National curriculum
Since 1988, the subjects taught in state sector schools in England and Wales have been prescribed as part of the National Curriculum. This is divided into four stages: key stages (KS) one and two relate to primary schools, whereas three and four are for secondary schools.

NVQs
This stands for National Vocational Qualification. These are for anyone aged 16 or over. They offer recognised vocational qualifications which are valued by employers because they demonstrate you have the high quality skills required at work.

Post-compulsory education
This refers to education which takes place after the school-leaving age of 16: that is, further education (ages 16 to 18) and higher education (university-level). In 2004/05 there were over 2.4 million students in further education and over 2.2 million in higher education in the UK.

School-leaving age
In the UK, the school-leaving age is 16: pupils are obliged by law to stay in school until this age. However, 73 per cent of post-compulsory education students in England stay on in further education until the age of 18.

Postgraduate
A postgraduate is a student who has completed their degree and gone on to further academic study, such as a PhD or Master's course.

Specialised diploma
A new qualification to recognise achievement at ages 14 to 19, the specialised diploma will be available for all from 2013. It will combine practical skill development with theoretical and technical understanding and knowledge.

Student debt
A higher education student can apply for a student loan from the government, which they begin paying back monthly after graduation once they are earning a certain salary. They may also incur additional debts such as overdrafts while at university. There are concerns that student debt is rising to unmanageable levels: recent research from NatWest suggest that new students can expect to pay £33,512 to get a degree.

Undergraduate
An undergraduate is a term applied to a student studying towards a first degree but who has not yet graduated.

INDEX